The Family & Human Life

Robert M. Haddad
Bernard Toutounji

Nihil Obstat: Rev. Peter Joseph, STD

Imprimatur: + Cardinal George Pell, Archbishop of Sydney

Date: 28th February, 2011

The *Nihil Obstat* and *Imprimatur* are a declaration that a book or pamphlet is considered to be free from doctrinal or moral error. It is not necessarily implied that those who have granted them agree with the contents, opinions or statements expressed.

Scripture quotes taken from the ***Revised Standard Version of the Bible (Catholic Edition)***, copyright © 1946, 1952, 1971, and the ***New Revised Standard Version of the Bible (Catholic Edition)***, copyright © 1989.

Extracts from *The Faith of the Early Fathers,* Rev. William A. Jurgens, copyright © 1970 by The Order of St. Benedict, Inc., The Liturgical Press, Collegeville, Minnesota. Used with permission.

Extracts from *The Roman Catechism*, Issued by order of Pope St Pius V, 1566, reprinted by TAN Books, Rockford, Illinois 61105.

Extracts from English translation of ***Catechism of the Catholic Church*** for Australia copyright © June 1994 St. Pauls/Libreria Editrice Vaticana. Used with permission.

Cover picture: Paul Mooney, Mooney Fine Art.

Printed by: Parousia Media; www.parousiamedia.com

© **Robert M. Haddad and Bernard Toutounji.** All rights reserved. Extracts and copies of various parts or chapters of the series may be made in cases of 'fair dealing', viz., for the purpose of teaching, promoting and defending the Catholic Faith. All acknowledgments given to **Robert M. Haddad and Bernard Toutounji.**

ISBN: 978-1-922660-62-6

To all those who endeavor to raise Christian families in today's world

Contents

Foreword	vii
Introduction	1
Man and Woman	4
Marriage	12
Children	21
The Family	28
Sexual Ethics	36
Transmission of Life	44
Reproductive Technology	52
Ethics of Life & Death	61
Appendix:	
Prayers	69
Internet Resources	72
Glossary	73
Special Thanks	81
About the Authors	82

Foreword

I have now lived long enough to witness many changes in the Church and in the world. The sexual revolution is certainly one event that has brought about many changes. It initially promised greater freedom and happiness, only to leave us with much less of both. We need to rediscover the tried and true certainties of the Gospel if we want to be authentically free and happy.

However, in today's social and political climate this is very difficult. The Church's gospel of life and love, as beautiful as it is, struggles to be heard above the noise and sirens of the alternative 'gospel' of license and promiscuity. Chastity, fidelity, abstinence are words not often heard in today's world.

Pope St John Paul II left us many great legacies, most particularly his teaching on love and sexuality, commonly known as *Theology of the Body*. While affirming traditional teachings, St John Paul II 're-packaged' Church teaching in a positive light, extolling the beauty and wonder of the human body and sexuality, highlighting their true meaning and purpose. Every effort must be made to proclaim *Theology of the Body* to today's young people.

Many attempts to present *Theology of the Body* to the world have already been successful, most notably the establishment of the *John Paul Institute for Marriage and the Family* in many countries, including Australia. The book *The Family and Human Life* is another step to address an important need. Written for younger people, it seeks to provide a solid introduction to the Church's teaching on critical matters relating to human happiness, including marriage, children, family, as well as the Church's response to the developing areas of reproductive technology and ethics of life and death. I am particularly pleased to see numerous quotations from the writings of modern-day Popes, including St John Paul II and Benedict XVI.

I wish to thank the authors, Robert Haddad and Bernard Toutounji, for their work in this project and hope that *The Family and Human Life* enjoys widespread circulation and success.

+ George Cardinal Pell, Archbishop of Sydney, April 2011

Introduction

"Ah, you who call evil good and good evil" (Is. 5:20).

Human beings are relational creatures. Of all the things humans need and desire the most important is love. All humans wish to love and be loved in return. Love is what drives humans to seek and enter into relationships.

One of the most common and important relationships is marriage. From marriage, new human life and families spring forth. Sex is part of the process and is therefore very important. We all want to know about it. But what should we know about marriage, sex, children and family life and from where should we learn it?

The Church is where most Catholics usually turn to for the answers to the big questions of life. In the past, Popes, bishops, priests, nuns and parents spoke the truth and provided solid answers to the big questions. The answers were usually provided without a great deal of explanation and amounted to a collection of "don'ts." This was fine in times when authority in the Church and society was generally respected and obeyed. However, things changed during the twentieth century. Something called the *sexual revolution* arrived. Authority and institutions everywhere began to be questioned and rejected.

The sexual revolution began in the 1920s and immediately presented a real challenge to prevailing mores. This challenge gathered momentum with World War Two, the development of mass media and the 'liberation' movements of the 1960s. At the beginning of the third millennium, the sexual revolution now comfortably sits hand in glove with other revolutionary movements seeking to advance a secular and atheist future for humanity.

The new revolutionary philosophy has as one of its slogans "God is dead" and its values can be summed up in the words of the Book of Wisdom: "For they reasoned unsoundly, saying to themselves, short and sorrowful is our life ... For we were born by mere chance, and hereafter we shall be as though we had never been ... Come, therefore, let us enjoy the good things that exist ... Let none of us fail to share in our revelry ... because this is our portion, and this our lot" (2:1-9).

Now, treading more boldly, the sexual revolution freely promotes all forms of permissiveness: pre-marital sex, contraception, abortion, sterilization, divorce, adultery, same-sex relationships, euthanasia, etc., under the banners of progress and freedom, while seeking legitimacy under the cloak of parliamentary majorities. The great moral decisions of humanity are now wholly subordinated to secular institutions that make no reference whatsoever to God or unchanging objective values.

The growing acceptance of moral evils in the mind of public opinion is a telling sign of the now extreme crisis of the moral sense, one that blurs the distinction between good and evil: "Ah, you who call evil good and good evil" (Is. 5:20). What has been the consequence?: "Man cannot abide in his pomp, he is like the beasts that perish. This is the fate of those who have foolish confidence, the end of those who are pleased with their portion" (Ps. 49:12-13).

Faced with the current social and moral crisis, the words of St Paul to St Timothy are very timely: "proclaim the message; be persistent whether the time is favorable or unfavorable; convince, rebuke, and encourage, with the utmost patience in teaching" (2 Tim. 4:2). Never has it been more critical than the present to state clearly the Church's teaching on marriage, sexuality and the family.

The Church's teachings on faith and morals can never change but they can *develop* over time. This is what Pope St John Paul II achieved with respect to marriage, sexuality etc. in his *Theology of the Body*, a series of teachings delivered in his Wednesday public audiences from 1979 to 1984. More than a knee-jerk reaction, St John Paul II's *Theology of the Body* is a well thought out and profound response to the sexual revolution. It is old wine in new wine skins, with a spot of new wine based on new discoveries about the human body.

Helping people to re-discover the truths about love and life – especially teenagers, young adults and married couples – is a critical priority for the Church today. The sexual revolution has failed to live up to its promises and has left humanity sadder rather than happier. Humanity deserves better. Humanity deserves a future built on goodness, truth and beauty, built on two thousand years of wisdom and experience derived from Jesus and the Apostles, built on St John Paul II's *Theology of the Body*.

Discussion Questions

1. What do humans need and desire more than anything else?

2. What do we mean by the 'sexual revolution'? What are some of its 'fruits'?

3. Has the sexual revolution been successful? In what ways?

4. How should the Church respond to the sexual revolution?

5. What do we mean by the *Theology of the Body*?

Activities

- Identify one contemporary television program which depicts marriage, sexuality and/or family life.

- Explain how marriage, sexuality and family life are presented in this television program.

- State how this presentation of marriage, sexuality and family life is consistent or inconsistent with Catholic beliefs.

Man and Woman

"So God created man in his own image, in the image of God he created him; male and female he created them" (Gen. 1:27); *"And the rib that the Lord God had taken from the man he made into a woman and brought her to the man"* (Gen. 2:22).

Equal in Dignity

Men and women share equally all the essential attributes of human nature. They are equally human beings, possess freedom and responsibility, have been redeemed by ur Lord Jesus Christ, and are destined for eternal glory and happiness.

All this can be gathered from Scripture. It is clear that the first woman was made not like the lower creatures but as a companion and helper to man "like himself": "It is not good that the man should be alone; I will make him a helper as his partner" (Gen. 2:18).

The pagan notion that the woman is an inferior kind of man has no place in the mind of Catholicism. The person of the Virgin Mary, the manner in which Jesus honored women, the role of women throughout our Savior's life, and the presence of women with the Apostles in the Upper Room on Pentecost Day, are vitally important facts concerning the status of women in Christian society:

> Therefore, Christ through His word which stands forever, elevated man in marriage and again raised up woman who had been cast down by the ancients to the role of slave and whom the most austere of the Roman censors had likened to 'an unbridled nature and an unsubdued animal'; just as the Redeemer had exalted in Himself not only man but woman, taking human nature from a woman and sublimating His Mother blessed among women, to an immaculate mirror of virtue and grace for every Christian family throughout the centuries, crowned in Heaven Queen of the Angels and Saints.[1]

---

[1] Pope Pius XII, *Address to Married Couples*, 22 April, 1942.

Complementary, not Contradictory

However, neither man nor woman possesses entirely all the plenitude of human qualities and powers. Their bodily structures are different, human personality manifests itself differently in each sex, and their physiological instincts and tendencies as well as their prevailing qualities of mind and character are not the same. Therefore, neither can be entirely representative of human nature. Rather, men and women are complementary to each other, forming an organic whole when united:

> The sexes, in keeping with the wonderful designs of the Creator, are destined to complement each other, in the family and in society, precisely because of their differences, which therefore ought to be maintained and encouraged.[2]

The complementary nature of men and women is ordered towards a higher end, namely, that they may together "live in truth and love":

> Male and female in their physical constitution, the two human subjects, even though physically different, share equally in the capacity to live 'in truth and love' ... their union ought to take place 'in truth and love', and thus express the maturity proper to persons created in the image and likeness of God.[3]

Much of what the Church teaches about the human person comes from the opening chapters of the book of Genesis. The creation account in Genesis chapter two begins with the first man being created by God from the "dust from the ground" (Gen. 2:7). This man only becomes a living being when God breathes into him "the breath of life." God infuses into man a spiritual soul, which is a created reflection of God's own life. The animals too are formed by God but are not given the same sharing in the divine life (cf. 2:19).

The original Hebrew text of Genesis refers to the first created human as *ha'adam*, which translates as 'the life-form' or the generic term

---

[2] Pope Pius XI, *Divini Illius Magistri, On the Christian Education of Youth*, 1929, #68.

[3] Pope St John Paul II, *Letter to Families*, 1994, #8.

'man.' Only after the creation of the first woman is *ha'adam* defined as a 'male.'[4]

With the shared acknowledgement of *ha'adam's* solitude by God and *ha'adam* (cf. Gen. 2:18 & 2:20), Scripture tells how God caused "a deep sleep" to fall upon the man and while he slept "he took one of his ribs and closed the flesh again in its place. With the rib that the Lord God had taken from the man he formed a woman" (Gen. 2:21-22).

At the end of this 're-creation', what emerges is no longer *ha'adam* but *'is'* (man-male) and *'issa'* (woman-female). Humanity is sexually awakened to a new unity and the original solitude of *ha'adam* is absorbed into a permanent desire for unity with the other sex. The creation of *'is'* and *'issa'*, two beings united in nature but different in sex, is "the 'definitive' creation of man." It can be said that solitude never did 'fit' mankind.[5]

Despite the differences between the bodies of men and women, the unity between the two beings is so evident that the woman is immediately accepted as the help suited to the man, and in the same way the woman, who has the same common memory of solitude, accepts the man as the companion she is longing for. It is their bodies that make the acceptance of each other possible; through the body of the other, they see the person and ultimately the communion they long for.

'Communion of Persons'

The term *Communio personarum* or 'communion of persons' was coined by Pope St John Paul II while attending the Second Vatican Council as Bishop Karol Wojytyla and was eventually inserted into the text of *Gaudium et Spes*:

> But God did not create man abandoning him alone, for from the beginning "male and female he created them" (Gen. 1:27), and their union constitutes the first form of the communion of persons [*communionis personarum*]. For by his innermost nature man is a social being and unless he relates himself to others he

---

[4] Pope St John Paul, *Theology of the Body*, 5:2.
[5] *Ibid.* 9:2.

can neither live nor develop his potential.[6]

In an authentic communion of persons both man and woman play different but equally important roles. Men are called to be husband and father and women are called to be wife and mother. Society is only weakened when men and women act in a way that is competitive or demeaning of the other.

Motherhood

One cannot understand the truth of a woman without understanding a woman's motherhood. Motherhood, as the fruit of the marital union, implies a unique openness:

> Motherhood involves a special communion with the mystery of life ... This unique contact with the new human being developing within her gives rise to an attitude towards human beings – not only towards her own child, but every human being – which profoundly marks the woman's personality. It is commonly thought that *women* are more capable than men of paying attention *to another person*, and that motherhood develops this predisposition even more.[7]

This 'other-centredness' has seen Catholic women engage in valuable work and study outside of the family home in all kinds of fields. Well-educated Catholic women have a vital role in raising and maintaining social ideals, purifying and balancing the political and legal systems, securing a more just administration of public affairs and improving public aid and benefits in support of the family.

The Church however, remains aware of the indispensable value of a woman's role as wife and mother and warns society against systems that do not honor this:

> The work of women in the home must be recognized and respected as something valuable and, indeed irreplaceable.

---

[6] Second Vatican Council, *Gaudium et Spes*, 1965, #12; Cf. *Catechism of the Catholic Church* #372.

[7] Pope St John Paul II, *Mulieris Dignitatem*, 1988, #18.

Hence, no woman should, in practice, be compelled to work outside the home; nor should one who works only in the home be less esteemed than one who works outside the home.[8]

Fatherhood

Men are also called to embrace their natural vocation as husbands and fathers. True marital love presupposes that a husband would have a profound respect for the equal dignity of his wife. Writing to men in the fourth century, St Ambrose stated:

> You are not her master, but her husband; she was not given to you to be your slave, but your wife ... Reciprocate her attentiveness to you and be grateful to her for her love.[9]

Men have a natural tendency and ability to lead and protect and fathers ought remember that their primary responsibility is the care and protection of their wife and children. The father is to watch over and love them with a love that would be ever willing to sacrifice his own life for them (cf. Eph. 5:25). The man is indeed the head of his family but this is a headship that is always modelled on and united with the headship of Christ, who came to serve and not to be served (cf. Mk 10:45).

A man's fatherhood should reveal and relive "the very fatherhood of God" which is a fatherhood that is always attentive and always present:

> Where social and cultural conditions so easily encourage a father to be less concerned with his family or at any rate less involved in the work of education, efforts must be made to restore socially the conviction that the place and task of the father in and for the family is of unique and irreplaceable importance. As experience teaches, the absence of a father causes psychological and moral imbalance and notable difficulties in family relationships, as does, in contrary circumstances, the oppressive presence of a father, especially where there still prevails the phenomenon of "machismo", or a wrong superiority of male prerogatives which humiliates women and inhibits the development of healthy family

---

[8] Pope St John Paul II, *Familiaris Consortio*, 1981, #23.
[9] St Ambrose of Milan, *Exameron*, 5, 7, 19 (c. AD 387).

relationships.[10]

Radical Feminism

The end of the twentieth century and the beginning of the twenty-first is witnessing an unprecedented onslaught by radical feminism and 'political correctness' to remold society. The radical feminist movement is essentially anti-Christian and naturalistic. It rigorously defends universal birth control, abortion on demand, free and easy divorce procedures, homosexuality, etc., while advocating a 'uni-sexism' that seeks the final abolition of all remaining legal and cultural distinctions between men and women. The Church continues to remind the world that true equality does not and never will mean an abolition of the differences between men and women, for these differences are good and willed by God:

> If social policies – in the areas of education, work, family, access to services and civic participation – must combat all unjust sexual discrimination, they must also listen to the aspirations and identify the needs of all. The defense and promotion of equal dignity and common personal values must be harmonized with attentive recognition of the difference and reciprocity between the sexes where this is relevant to the realization of one's humanity, whether male or female.[11]

---

[10] *Familiaris Consortio* #25.
[11] Congregation for the Doctrine of the Faith, *On the Collaboration of Men and Women in the Church and in the World*, 2004, #14.

The Fathers

St Ambrose of Milan, *Paradise* 10, 48 (c. AD 375)

"Nor is it a matter of indifference that the woman was not formed of the same clay from which Adam was made, but was made from the rib of Adam himself, so that we might know that the flesh of man and woman is of but one nature, and that there is but one source of the human race. Therefore at the beginning it is not two that are made, man and woman, nor two men, nor two women, but first man is made, and then woman from him. For God willed to settle one nature upon mankind, and starting from the one origin of this creature, He snatched away the possibility of numerous and disparate natures."

The Roman Catechism (1566)

Pt. II, Ch. VIII: It should not be forgotten that Eve was called by Adam *his companion. The woman*, he says, *whom thou gavest me as a companion.* Hence it was, according to the opinion of some of the holy Fathers, that she was formed not from the feet but from the side of man; as, on the other hand, she was not formed from his head, in order to give her to understand that it was not hers to command but to obey her husband.

Catechism of the Catholic Church (1992)

No. 371: God created man and woman *together* and willed each *for* the other. The Word of God gives us to understand this through various features of the sacred text. "It is not good that the man should be alone. I will make him a helper fit for him." None of the animals can be man's partner. The woman God "fashions" from the man's rib and brings to him elicits on the man's part a cry of wonder, an exclamation of love and communion: "This at last is bone of my bones and flesh of my flesh." Man discovers woman as another "I", sharing the same humanity.

Discussion Questions

1. What is meant by the term 'image of God'?

2. In contrast to paganism, how did Christianity elevate the status of women?

3. How are men and women the same/different?

4. What do we understand by the term 'communion of persons'?

5. Why should Christians be concerned about 'radical feminism'?

Activities

- Conduct a class debate:

    "In an authentic communion of persons both man and woman play different but equally important roles."

- Divide the class/group into affirmative and negative.

- Allow ten-twenty minutes to identify and discuss points which support or oppose the above statement.

Marriage

"For this reason a man will leave his father and mother and be joined to his wife, and the two will become one flesh" (Eph. 5:31).

Vocation and Covenant

Marriage, as taught by the Catholic Church throughout the ages, is an irrevocable covenant involving God, one man and one woman, instituted for the good of the spouses and ordained for the birth and education of children for God:

> By their very nature, the institution of matrimony itself and conjugal love are ordained for the procreation and education of children, and it is in them that it finds its crowning glory.[1]

In forming the covenantal bond, the man and woman exchange not *something* but *everything*, not *things* but *themselves*. In the process they become "one flesh" (Gen. 2:24). This unity is also a community, reflecting the community of love within God Himself, Father, Son and Holy Spirit. Furthermore, as the love between the Father and the Son is fruitful in the procession of the Holy Spirit, similarly the covenantal love between the husband and wife achieves fruitfulness in the begetting of children.

Unlike ancient heretical sects such as the Gnostics, Christianity has always esteemed marriage as a great good, a holy state blessed by God and commended by Christ Himself. Marriage is the vocation to which the vast majority of humanity is called. Hence, St Paul declares marriage to be "a great mystery" (Eph. 5:32), "held in honor by all" (Heb. 13:4).

The fact that marriage was established and blessed directly by God is plain from the account of the first marriage between Adam and Eve:

> "And the rib that the Lord God had taken from the man he made into a woman and brought her to the man. Then the man said, 'This at last is bone of my bones and flesh of my flesh; this one

---

[1] Second Vatican Council, *Gaudium et Spes*, 1965, #48.

shall be called Woman, for out of Man this one was taken.' Therefore a man leaves his father and his mother and clings to his wife, and they become one flesh" (Gen. 2:22-24).

Not only was marriage instituted by God, the union between man and woman was from the beginning a foreshadowing of the union between Christ and His Church:

> "Husbands, love your wives, just as Christ loved the church and gave himself up for her, in order to make her holy by cleansing her with the washing of water by the word, so as to present the church to himself in splendor, without a spot or wrinkle or anything of the kind – yes, so that she may be holy and without blemish. In the same way, husbands should love their wives as they do their own bodies" (Eph. 5:25-28).

> Christ the Lord abundantly blessed this many-faceted love, welling up as it does from the fountain of divine love and structured as it is on the model of His union with the Church ... He abides with them thereafter so that, just as He loved the Church and handed Himself over on her behalf, the spouses may love each other with perpetual fidelity through mutual self-bestowal.[2]

Jesus Christ elevated marriage to the dignity of a sacrament, thus restoring it to the original integrity it possessed before the Fall. Catholics cannot validly enter the marital covenant without receiving the sacrament for it consecrates the union by conferring sanctifying grace and bestows supernatural aids on the parties to bring forth "citizens with the saints and also members of the household of God" (Eph. 2:19) and to "render mutual help and service to each other through an intimate union of their persons and of their actions."[3]

---

[2] *Gaudium et Spes* #48.
[3] *Ibid.*

Marital Consent

For the marriage covenant to be validly formed the man and woman must be prepared to vow and live out the characteristics of married love, namely, freely embraced, totally given, faithful unto death and open to the gift of life.[4] This free, total, faithful and fruitful consent constitutes the form of the sacrament of Holy Matrimony.

By "freely embraced" is meant an act of the will in union with the senses so that it is a fully human consent able to endure and grow in the midst of the everyday vicissitudes of life. By "totally given" is meant a consent in which husband and wife intend to generously share everything, without reservations or selfish calculations. By "faithful" is meant a consent given by the bride and groom that excludes all others until death. Only such a love provides profound and lasting happiness. By "fruitful" is meant a consent intending to raise up new lives as the supreme gift of marriage.

By the words of consent the man and woman minister to one another the gift of themselves. In this free act a supernatural bond is placed around the couple "so that they are no longer two, but one flesh" (Mt 19:6). *Gaudium et Spes* speaks of spouses being "fortified" and "consecrated" for the "duties and dignity" of their state.[5] It is in their marriage that couples "increasingly further their own perfection and their mutual sanctification, and together they render glory to God."[6]

The words of consent also have another vitally important function, namely, to "define the common good of the couple and of the family":

> First, the common good of the spouses: love, fidelity, honor, the permanence of their union until death - 'all the days of my life.' The good of both, which is at the same time the good of each, must then become the good of the children. The common good, by its very nature, both unites individual persons and ensures the true good of each.[7]

---

[4] Pope Paul VI, *Humanae Vitae*, 1968, #9.
[5] *Gaudium et Spes* #48.
[6] *Ibid.*
[7] Pope St John Paul II, *Letter to Families*, 1994, #10.

The Christian ideal of marriage can be summed up in the following formula: *"One with one, exclusively and forever."* Hence, Christian marriage excludes polygamy, where a man has more than one wife; and polyandry, where a woman has more than one husband. Likewise, all actions, words, etc., which would turn the marriage vows of a couple into a lie, are equally prohibited to both husband and wife.

Divorce

As a result of this understanding of marriage, all possibility of divorce is excluded. While in some cases the *separation* of spouses – while maintaining the marriage bond – can be legitimate, the Church has no power to dissolve "a ratified and consummated marriage ... for any reason other than death."[8] Divorce is destructive of the ends of marriage and opens the floodgates of immorality. Though it was tolerated under the Law of Moses, Jesus, perfecting that same Law, categorically abolished it, reminding all of God's original intention for this sacred union:

> *"Have you not read that he who made them from the beginning made them male and female, and said, 'For this reason a man shall leave his father and mother and be joined to his wife, and the two shall become one flesh?' So they are no longer two but one flesh. What therefore God has joined together, let not man put asunder." They said to him, "Why then did Moses command one to give a certificate of divorce, and to put her away?" Jesus said to them, "For your hardness of heart Moses allowed you to divorce your wives, but from the beginning it was not so"* (Mt 19:4-8).

A couple may be civilly divorced to make the necessary legal arrangements when they separate but they must understand that they are still married in the sight of God (unless a Church tribunal has declared the marriage null and void).

Only where the *Pauline Privilege* operates is separation and remarriage allowed. In the case where one member of an unbaptized couple converts and is baptized, and the other partner inhibits the

---

[8] *Code of Canon Law*, Canon 1141.

practice of the convert's faith, the baptized partner is free to leave the unbaptized spouse and marry again (1 Cor. 7:12-15).

Annulments

Annulments are distinguishable from dissolution of marriage in that they are pronouncements by the Church that there *never existed a valid marriage in the first place*. To be declared null, it must be ascertained that some essential element was absent at the time of marriage. Grounds for annulment include, for example: psychological incapacity; consent extracted through force or fear; deceit or fraud perpetrated to secure consent; an intention to have no children; an intention to exclude fidelity or permanence.

Headship

In respect of the primary marital rights and obligations, husband and wife are equal. Nevertheless, since the family forms a true society the natural and divine law has designated the man to be its governing head:

> "Wives, be subject to your husbands as you are to the Lord. For the husband is the head of the wife just as Christ is the head of the church, the body of which he is the Savior. Just as the church is subject to Christ, so also wives ought to be, in everything, to their husbands" (Eph. 5:22-24).

> The man is the ruler of the family and the head of the woman; but because she is flesh of his flesh and bone of his bone, let her be subject and obedient to the man, not as a servant but as a companion, so that nothing be lacking of honor or of dignity in the obedience which she gives.[9]

Pope Pius XI explains the limits to this subjection:

> This subjection, however, does not deny or take away the liberty which fully belongs to the woman both in view of her dignity as a

---

[9] Pope Leo XIII, *Arcanum Divinae*, 1880, #11.

human person, and in view of her most noble office as wife and mother and companion; nor does it bid her obey her husband's every request, if not in harmony with right reason or with the dignity due to a wife ... In fact if the husband neglect his duty, it falls to the wife to take his place in directing the family. But the structure of the family and its fundamental law, established and confirmed by God, must always and everywhere remain intact.[10]

Pope St John Paul II in his catechesis on the *Theology of the Body* also examines the Ephesians text, stating that the 'submission' spoken of must always be firstly a mutual submission to Christ. However, although both are called to a submission ...

> The husband is above all the one who loves and the wife by contrast, is the one who is loved. One might even venture the idea that the wife's 'submission' to the husband ... means above all 'the experiencing of love.' This is all the more so, because this 'submission' refers to the image of the submission of the Church to Christ, which certainly consists in experiencing his love.[11]

Being aware of the challenges that marriage faces in modern society, the Church continues to proclaim to the world that marriage is an institution beyond personal manipulation as its foundations lie in the truth of man and of his destiny. It is only in self-giving that human persons discover the joy for which they were created:

> How is it possible to communicate the beauty of marriage to the people of today? We see how many young people are reluctant to marry in church because they are afraid of finality; indeed, they are even reluctant to have a civil wedding. Today, too many young people and even to some who are not so young, definitiveness appears as a constriction, a limitation of freedom. And what they want first of all is freedom. They are afraid that in the end they might not succeed. They see so many failed marriages. They fear that this juridical form, as they understand it, will be an external weight that will extinguish love.

---

[10] Pope Pius XI, *Casti Connubii*, 1930, #27.
[11] Pope St John Paul II, *Theology of the Body*, 92:6.

It is essential to understand that it is not a question of a juridical bond, a burden imposed with marriage. On the contrary, depth and beauty lie precisely in finality. Only in this way can love mature to its full beauty.[12]

Celibacy and Virginity

Though marriage is a necessary gift for the human race as a whole, Jesus spoke of those who would set aside the good of marriage "for the sake of the kingdom of heaven" (Mt 19:12). While a life of celibacy undertaken for God's glory is never to be understood as a "disparagement of marriage"[13] the Church has always viewed it as possessing an objectively higher excellence: "So that he who marries his betrothed does well; and he who refrains from marriage will do better" (1 Cor. 7:38). Virginity for the sake of the Kingdom is an unfolding of baptismal grace, a powerful sign of the supremacy of the bond with Christ and a reminder that marriage is a reality of this present age which is passing away.[14] A life of celibacy implies a more complete self-denial, more opportunities for prayer and closer union with God, and a closer imitation of Christ's very own life:

> ... according to the teaching of the Church holy virginity surpasses marriage in excellence ... Virginity is preferable to marriage then as we have said, above all else because it is a higher aim; that is to say, it is a most efficacious way or means of devoting oneself wholly to the service of God, while the heart of the married person will always remain more or less divided.[15]

> Let them perceive as well the superiority of virginity consecrated to Christ, so that by a choice which is maturely thought out and magnanimous they may attach themselves to God by a total gift of body and soul.[16]

---

[12] Pope Benedict XVI, *Meeting with the priests of the Diocese of Albano*, 31 August, 2006.
[13] *Theology of the Body*, 77:6.
[14] *Catechism of the Catholic Church* #1619.
[15] Pope Pius XII, *Sacra Virginitas*, 1954, #24.
[16] Second Vatican Council, *Decree on Priestly Formation*, 1965, #10.

The Fathers

St Augustine of Hippo, *On the Good of Marriage* 24 (AD 401)

"These are the goods because of which marriages are considered good: children, fidelity, and sacrament ... The good of marriage among all nations and among all men consists in the cause of generation and the fidelity of chastity. When there is question of the people of God, however, another good can also be found: the sanctity or sacredness of the sacrament."

The Roman Catechism (1566)

Pt. II, Ch. VIII: Matrimonial fidelity also demands that they love one another with a special, holy and pure love; not as adulterers love one another but as Christ loves His Church. This is the rule laid down by the Apostle when he says: *Husbands, love your wives as Christ also loved the church.* And surely (Christ's) love for His Church was immense; it was a love inspired not by His own advantage, but also by the advantage of His spouse.

Catechism of the Catholic Church (1992)

No. 1604: God who created man out of love also calls him to love the fundamental and innate vocation of every human being. For man is created in the image and likeness of God who is himself love. Since God created him man and woman, their mutual love becomes an image of the absolute and unfailing love with which God loves man. It is good, very good, in the Creator's eyes. And this love which God blesses is intended to be fruitful and to be realized in the common work of watching over creation: "And God blessed them, and God said to them: 'Be fruitful and multiply, and fill the earth and subdue it.'"

Discussion Questions

1. Define marriage.

2. What are the two 'ends' of marriage?

3. The marriage relationship foreshadows which other relationship?

4. What is necessary to form a valid marriage covenant?

5. What does a life of celibacy or virginity imply?

Activities

- Obtain a copy of the *Rite of Marriage* and locate the words of 'consent'.

- Discuss the meaning of the word 'consent'.

- Describe what the couple are 'consenting to' in the Marriage Rite.

- Would you agree that the 'consent' is a very important part of the Marriage Rite? Why/Why not?

Children

"Sons are indeed a heritage from the Lord, the fruit of the womb a reward. Like arrows in the hand of a warrior are the sons of one's youth. Happy is the man who has his quiver full of them. He shall not be put to shame when he speaks with his enemies in the gate" (Ps. 127:3-5).

A 'Good' of Marriage

The Church has always taught that there are three principal 'goods' of marriage: fidelity, the sacrament, and children. Having regard to these, the Second Vatican Council observed that marriage and love find their "ultimate crown" in the birth and education of children:

> By their very nature, the institution of matrimony itself and conjugal love are ordained for the procreation and education of children, and find in them their ultimate crown.[1]

As the marriage union is willed by God to perpetuate the human race through the birth and education of children, nature ordains the continued union of the parents after the child's birth and the unity of the parents and children in one closely-knit society:

> (I)n marriage provision has been made in the best possible way for the education of children that is so necessary, for, since the parents are bound together by an indissoluble bond, the care and mutual help of each is always at hand.[2]

Mutual Rights and Obligations

Within this society there are imposed upon both parents and children mutual rights and obligations. On the part of parents they include to love, protect, discipline and assist their children in all their

---

[1] Second Vatican Council, *Gaudium et Spes*, 1965, #48.
[2] Pope Pius XI, *Casti Connubii*, 1930, #11.

spiritual and corporal needs. Children for their part are to love, obey and show gratitude to their parents for their support during the period of their infancy and the many years of their upbringing: "Honor your father and mother – this is the first commandment with a promise: so that it may be well with you and you may live long on the earth" (Eph. 6:2-3).

The parents' authority over their children is limited by the natural and divine law. Consequently, it would not include the power of life or death or the right to sell them, or to impose unjust or inhumane conditions upon them.

> In the family, which is a community of persons, special attention must be devoted to the children by developing a profound esteem for their personal dignity, and a great respect and generous concern for their rights. This is true for every child, but it becomes all the more urgent the smaller the child is and the more it is in need of everything, when sick, suffering or handicapped.[3]

Naturally, parental authority becomes less stringent and comprehensive as the children begin to take care of themselves and it ceases upon their reaching adulthood. Furthermore, parents cannot interfere with the natural rights of their children to choose their own vocation after they have reached their majority. They can advise and direct, but not command:

> Children should be so educated that as adults they can, with a mature sense of responsibility, follow their vocation, including a religious one, and choose their state of life ... At the same time no pressure, direct or indirect, should be put on the young to make them enter marriage or choose a specific partner.[4]

Education

Education as understood from the Church's point of view is the collection of all those cares and activities by which the child's physical, mental and moral faculties are developed. Parents have the most solemn obligation to educate their offspring and nothing can compensate for

---

[3] Pope St John Paul II, *Familiaris Consortio*, 1981, #26.
[4] *Gaudium et Spes* #52.

their failure to do so: "to die childless is better than to have ungodly children" (Sir. 16:3). The family is the first school of all the moral and social virtues:

> Since parents have given children their life, they are bound by the most serious obligation to educate their offspring and therefore must be recognized as the primary and principal educators ... The family is the first school of the social virtues that every society needs. It is particularly in the Christian family, enriched by the grace and office of the sacrament of matrimony, that children should be taught from their early years to have a knowledge of God according to the faith received in Baptism, to worship Him, and to love their neighbor. Here, too, they find their first experience of a wholesome human society and of the Church. Finally, it is through the family that they are gradually led to a companionship with their fellowmen and with the people of God.[5]

It is consequently contrary to Church teaching to suggest that children belong to the State rather than the family or that the State has an absolute right over their education:

> The right of parents to choose an education in conformity with their religious faith must be absolutely guaranteed.[6]

Parents must create a family atmosphere that is animated with love and reverence for God and neighbor.[7] Children must be thoroughly instructed and habituated in the practice of the Faith. In doing so, parents become the first heralds of the Gospel to their children:

> As a result, with parents leading the way by example and family prayer, children and indeed everyone gathered around the family hearth will find a readier path to human maturity, salvation, and holiness. Graced with the dignity and office of fatherhood and motherhood, parents will energetically acquit themselves of the

---

[5] Second Vatican Council, *Gravissimum Educationis*, 1965, #3.
[6] *Familiaris Consortio* #40.
[7] Cf. *Catechism of the Catholic Church* #2223.

duty which devolves primarily on them, namely education, and especially religious education.[8]

Education in Sexuality

One of the most vital yet most neglected areas of the education that parents need to provide for their children is with regard to formation in the true meaning of sexuality. Whereas in the past the general culture was permeated by respect for fundamental values, such is no longer the case, and many children have been left to fend for themselves with parents unprepared and unequipped to provide adequate guidance.

The Church recognizes chastity - "the spiritual power with frees love from selfishness" - as the foundational principle in all education in sexuality. In 1995, the Pontifical Council for the Family published a comprehensive document entitled *"The Truth and Meaning of Human Sexuality"*, which provides parents with a comprehensive set of principles for education in sexuality within the family. This document outlined four general principles to guide parents in this important work:

1) *Each child is a unique and unrepeatable person and must receive individualized formation.* The Church reminds all those involved in education that it is the parents who are in the best position to know what is suitable for each of their children and when and how to impart individualized formation.
2) *The moral dimension must always be a part of their explanations.* Parents should stress that Christians are called to live the gift of sexuality according the plan of God who is Love.
3) *Formation in chastity and timely information regarding sexuality must be provided in the broadest context of education for love.* In addition to information about sex and objective moral principles parents must expose their children to the means by which they can best practise a healthy and chaste sexuality, namely, frequent use of the sacraments, prudence, control of the senses, etc.
4) *Parents should provide this information with great delicacy, but clearly and at the appropriate time.* Parents should seek light from God in

---

[8] *Gaudium et Spes* #48.

Children

prayer and through discussion with one another to ensure that throughout the growth of their children they impart the correct information at the correct times.[9]

The Church reminds parents that amidst the challenges of educating children in Christian chastity they always have, through the sacrament of their own marriage, all the gifts of grace to enable them to work with God in forming solid foundations for their children:

> Much of the formation in the home is indirect, incarnated in a loving and tender atmosphere, for it arises from the presence and example of parents whose love is pure and generous. If parents are given confidence in this task of education for love, they will be inspired to overcome the challenges and problems of our times by their own ministry of love.[10]

---

[9] Pontifical Council for the Family, *The Truth and Meaning of Human Sexuality*, 1995, ##65-76.
[10] *Ibid.* #149.

The Fathers

St Augustine of Hippo, *On the Good of Marriage* 9 (AD 401)

"Truly we must consider, that God gives us some goods, which are to be sought for their own sake, such as wisdom, health, friendship ... For of these, certain are necessary for the sake of wisdom, as learning: certain for the sake of health, as meat and drink and sleep: certain for the sake of friendship, as marriage or sexual intercourse: for hence subsists the propagation of the human kind, wherein friendly fellowship is a great good ... and on this account it is good to marry, because it is good to beget children, to be a mother of a family."

The Roman Catechism (1566)

Pt. II, Ch. VIII: The first blessing, then, is family, that is to say, children born of a true and lawful wife. So highly did the Apostle esteem this blessing that he says: *The woman shall be saved by bearing children.* These words are to be understood not only of bearing children, but also of bringing them up and training them to the practice of piety; for the Apostle immediately subjoins: *If she continue in faith.* Scripture says: *Hast thou children? Instruct them and bow down their necks from childhood.* The same is taught by the Apostle; while Tobias, Job and other holy Patriarchs in Sacred Scripture furnish us with beautiful examples of such training.

Catechism of the Catholic Church (1992)

No. 2226: *Education in the faith* by the parents should begin in the child's earliest years. This already happens when family members help one another to grow in faith by the witness of a Christian life in keeping with the Gospel. Family catechesis precedes, accompanies, and enriches other forms of instruction in the faith. Parents have the mission of teaching their children to pray and to discover their vocation as children of God. The parish is the Eucharistic community and the heart of the liturgical life of Christian families; it is a privileged place for the catechesis of children and parents.

Discussion Questions

1. What is the principal purpose of marriage?

2. What are the mutual rights and obligations of parents and children?

3. What are some of the limits to parental authority?

4. What kind of family atmosphere ought parents to create?

5. What are the four principles to guide parents in educating their children in sexuality?

Activities

- List the four most important things that Christian parents should teach their children.

- Give reasons as to why these four areas are so important.

- How would you convey this message to Christian parents?

The Family

"Unless the Lord builds the house, those who build it labour in vain" (Ps. 127:1)

The Importance of the Family

The family is, by nature, the fundamental building block of society, the institution designed for the continuance and development of the human race. The importance of the family was clearly recognized by the Second Vatican Council:

> The well-being of the individual person and of human and Christian society is intimately linked with the healthy condition of that community produced by marriage and family.[1]

Though small in itself, the family constitutes a true society, with its own head and members, rights and obligations:

> The family is a society limited, indeed, in numbers, but no less a true society, anterior to every kind of state or nation, invested with rights and duties of its own, totally independent of the civil community ... governed by a power within its limits, that is, the father.[2]

The family is said to be 'the path of Christians', common and unique at the same time. According to Pope St John Paul II,

> It is a path common to all, yet one which is particular, unique and unrepeatable, just as every individual is unrepeatable; it is a path from which man cannot withdraw.[3]

---

[1] *Gaudium et Spes*, 1965, #47.
[2] Pope Leo XIII, *Rerum Novarum*, 1891, #9.
[3] *Letter to Families*, 1994, #2.

The Church looks to the family and recalls that Christ grew up in the family of Mary and Joseph and that in the early Church whole households were baptized together; it was these families that were "islands of Christian life in an unbelieving world."[4] In fact, it can be said that the Church "is nothing other than the 'family of God.'"[5] Without believing families there can be no people of God from which the faith radiates to others.

'Communion of Persons'

The family lives in a unity that reflects the very life of the Trinity.[6] As humans are created in the image and likeness of God, the family of father, mother and children transcend mere biological links; they form the first human society that is "completely pervaded by the very essence of 'communion.'"[7] Hence the term *communio personarum* (communion of persons), commonly used to describe the family by the Church since the Second Vatican Council. As a reflection of the divine family, it is the model of husband, wife and children that should be considered "the normal reference point" by which different forms of family relationships "are to be evaluated."[8] In *Christifideles Laici*, Pope St John Paul II wrote that in confronting modern anti-life and corrupt ideologies the family would continue to be "the primary place of 'humanization' for the person and society."[9]

Defending the Family

The family in modern times is under great attack, threatened by many forces that seek to destroy or deform it. It is incumbent on all Christians to uphold and defend the concept of the 'traditional family':

---

[4] *Catechism of the Catholic Church* #1655.
[5] *Ibid.*
[6] Cf. *Catechism of the Catholic Church* #2205.
[7] *Letter to Families* #7.
[8] *Catechism of the Catholic Church* #2202.
[9] *Christifideles Laici*, 1988, #40.

At a moment of history in which the family is the object of numerous forces that seek to destroy it or in some way to deform it, and aware that the well-being of society and her own good are intimately tied to the good of the family, the Church perceives in a more urgent and compelling way her mission of proclaiming to all people the plan of God for marriage and the family, ensuring their full vitality and human and Christian development, and thus contributing to the renewal of society and of the People of God.[10]

Pope Benedict XVI, speaking early in his Pontificate to a diocesan convention in Rome, continued the magisterial commitment and focus on the family:

> ... not only because today this fundamental human reality (the family) is subjected to a multitude of problems and threats and is therefore especially in need of evangelization and practical support, but also because Christian families constitute a crucial resource for education in the faith, for the edification of the Church as communion and for her ability to be a missionary presence in the most varied situations of life, as well as to act as a Christian leaven in the widespread culture and social structures.[11]

Due to its pivotal role, the family is also said to be prior to the State, for without the family as its principle and foundation, the State would not properly exist. Hence, it is the obligation of the State to promote and protect the well being of the family:

> ... if the family finds itself in exceeding distress ... it is right that extreme necessity be met by public aid, since each family is a part of the commonwealth. In like manner, if, within the precincts of the household, there should occur grave disturbance of mutual rights, public authority should intervene to force each party to yield to the other its proper due.[12]

---

[10] Pope St John Paul II, *Familiaris Consortio*, 1981, #3.
[11] Pope Benedict XVI, *"Address of his Holiness Benedict XVI to the participants in the Ecclesial Diocesan Convention of Rome"*, 2005.
[12] *Letter to Families* #2.

Those who have the care of the State and of the common good cannot neglect the needs of married people without bringing great harm upon the State and upon the common welfare ... Not only in those things which regard temporal goods is it the concern of public authority that proper provision be made for matrimony and the family, but also in matters pertaining to the good of souls.[13]

The Rights of the Family

The Church has taken upon itself the task of outlining the rights of the family in the religious, moral, social and material fields[14]:

(i) All persons have the right to choose their state of life and thus to marry and establish a family or to remain single.
(ii) Marriage cannot be contracted without the free and full consent of the spouses duly expressed.
(iii) The spouses have the inalienable right to found a family.
(iv) Human life must be respected and protected absolutely from the moment of conception.
(v) Parents have the original, primary and inalienable right to educate their children.
(vi) The family has the right to exist and to progress as a family.
(vii) Every family has the right to live freely, profess publicly and to propagate the Faith.
(viii) The family has the right to exercise its social and political functions in society.
(ix) Families have the right to adequate public assistance in the juridical, economic, social and fiscal domains.
(x) Families have a right to conditions of work which do not hinder the unity, well-being, health and stability of family life.
(xi) The family has the right to decent housing and basic services.
(xii) The families of migrants have the right to the same protection as that accorded other families.

---

[13] Pope Pius XI, *Casti Connubii*, 1930, #123.
[14] Pontifical Council for the Family, *Charter of the Rights of the Family*, 1983.

As history attests, where there is a weakening of the family there follows the disintegration of society. Civil laws should secure as far as possible the strengthening of family ties, the free operation of the laws of God in their regard, and the discouragement of all temptation to their violation:

> The prosperity of the State and the temporal happiness of its citizens cannot remain safe and sound where the foundations upon which they are established, which is the moral order, is weakened, and where the very fountain-head from which the State draws its life, namely, wedlock and the family is obstructed by the vices of its citizens.[15]

The 'Domestic Church'

It is within families that all the social and moral virtues are taught and passed on. Likewise, it is the depository of the local and national traditions of a people, as well as the mainstay of a sound economic system. The fruits of a good Christian home as the "domestic Church" consequently overflow to bring benefit to the whole of society:

> Each Christian family presents a likeness of the heavenly home; and the wondrous benefits thence resulting are not limited simply to the family circle, but spread abroad abundantly over the State at large.[16]

> From this marriage, in fact, comes the family, in which new citizens of human society are born, who by the grace of God received with baptism become children of God and perpetuate through the ages his own people. In this, which can be called the domestic Church, the parents must be for their children the first teachers of the faith, and foster the vocation proper to each, and that to religion with special care.[17]

Therefore, to the extent to which the Christian family accepts the Gospel and matures in faith it becomes an evangelizing

---

[15] *Casti Connubii* #123.
[16] Pope Leo XIII, *Quod Apostolici Muneris*, 1878, #8.
[17] Second Vatican Council, *Lumen Gentium*, 1964, #11.

community ... It is truly a service to the Church, to the building-up of the one Body of Christ ... Indeed, the Christian family is called upon, by its example and witness, to enlighten all those who seek the truth.[18]

Scripture speaks boldly on the obligations of the family as the domestic Church:

> "No, for I have chosen him, that he may charge his children and his household after him to keep the way of the Lord by doing righteousness and justice" (Gen. 18:19).

> "Your children are also to be commanded to do what is right and to give alms, and to be mindful of God and to bless his name at all times with sincerity and with all their strength" (Tob. 14:8).

> "And whoever does not provide for relatives, and especially for family members, has denied the faith and is worse than an unbeliever" (1 Tim. 5:8).

---

[18] Ibid. Cf. *Catechism of the Catholic Church* #1656.

The Fathers

St John Chrysostom, *Homilies on Genesis* 7, 1 (inter AD 386-395)

"When yesterday I said, 'each one of you must see to it that your home becomes a Church', you responded in loud voices and were pleased at what like words had produced in you."

The Roman Catechism (1566)

Pt. II, Ch. VIII: The husband should also be constantly occupied in some honest pursuit with a view to provide necessities for the support of his family and to avoid idleness, the root of almost every vice ... He is also to keep all his family in order, to correct their morals, and to see that they faithfully discharge their duties.

The wife should love to remain at home ... To train their children in the practice of virtue and to pay particular attention to their domestic concerns should also be especial objects of their attention.

Catechism of the Catholic Church (1992)

No. 2685: The *Christian family* is the first place of education in prayer. Based on the sacrament of marriage, the family is the "domestic church" where God's children learn to pray "as the Church" and to persevere in prayer. For young children in particular, daily family prayer is the first witness of the Church's living memory as awakened patiently by the Holy Spirit.

Discussion Questions

1. Why is the family a true society?

2. What is meant by the term 'traditional family'?

3. Why is the family 'prior' to the State?

4. What are some of the rights of the family in the religious, moral, social and material fields?

5. What is meant by the term 'Domestic Church'?

Activities

- Conduct a class conversation:

  Pope St John Paul II wrote that the family is the primary place of 'humanization' for the person and society.

  Imagine a society where family no longer existed. Where and how would the individual learn to be 'human'? What would this type of society look like?

Sexual Ethics

"Do you not know that your body is a temple of the Holy Spirit within you, which you have from God, and that you are not your own? For you were bought with a price; therefore glorify God in your body" (1 Cor. 6:15-20).

The 'sexual revolution' of the 1960's brought about a profound and devastating collapse in the morals of Western society. Today, the corruption has reached such an extent that we witness nothing less than a worldwide exaltation of illicit sex invading virtually every field of human life. In literature, films, news, advertizing and the internet, licence to practice any and every form of sexual activity is preached without end, while those who wish to live the Church's teaching on sexuality are either silenced, ridiculed and derided as out of touch and out of date.

Chastity

Chastity (often wrongly confused with celibacy) is at its most basic level the response of the human person to his or her creation in the likeness of God:

> God is love and in Himself He lives a mystery of personal loving communion. Creating the human race in His own image and continually keeping it in being, God inscribed in the humanity of man and woman the vocation, and thus the capacity and responsibility, of love and communion.[1]

Chastity is what allows men and women to express love so as to allow them to enter into genuine communion either in marriage, virginity or celibacy. Chastity is the integration of the sexuality of a person; it stops a person from descending to the level of brute animals where all importance is in the physical, or, ascending to the level of angels where all importance is in the spiritual. As man is a composite of body and soul he can only experience happiness when he loves with his whole being and is

---

[1] Pope St John Paul II, *Familiaris Consortio*, 1981, #11.

in control of that whole being. It is for this reason that the Church regards chastity as one of the most important virtues to be acquired:

> Chastity includes an apprenticeship in self-mastery which is a training in human freedom. The alternative is clear: either man governs his passions and finds peace, or he lets himself be dominated by them and becomes unhappy.[2]

All persons are called, whatever their specific vocation, to practise chastity in their everyday lives. Those who have professed virginity or consecrated celibacy live out chastity by giving themselves solely to God, thereby making themselves available in a unique way to the service of God and His people. Those who are married live out conjugal chastity by loving one another in a way that is always honest. Those who are engaged to marry or are still single live chastity in continence, always responsive to the hand of God in their lives.

Growing in self-mastery and chastity is the work of a lifetime and requires renewed effort at each stage of life. While growth in chastity is a personal task for each individual, there are certain norms which need to be a part of every Christian's life. These include the avoidance of occasions of sin, observing modesty in dress, wholesome recreation, daily prayer and frequent reception of the sacraments of Holy Communion and Penance. "Young people especially should earnestly foster devotion to the Immaculate Mother of God, and take as examples the lives of the Saints and other faithful people, especially young ones, who excelled in the practice of chastity."[3]

Masturbation

It is said by a myriad of modern-day psychologists and sociologists that masturbation is a normal part of sexual development and hence not a serious fault. However, whatever the extent to which masturbation is practised, particularly by the young, it is always "an intrinsically and

---

[2] *Catechism of the Catholic Church* #2339.
[3] Sacred Congregation for the Doctrine of the Faith, *Persona Humana, Declaration on Certain Questions Concerning Sexual Ethics*, 1975, #12.

seriously disordered act" which "contradicts the finality of the faculty."[4] The use of the sexual faculty must always be in the context of the marriage as it is only in such a relationship that the genuine meaning of self-giving worth can be achieved.

> On the subject of masturbation modern psychology provides much valid and useful information for formulating a more equitable judgment on moral responsibility and for orienting pastoral action. Psychology helps one to see how the immaturity of adolescence (which can sometimes persist after that age), psychological imbalance or habit can influence behaviour, diminishing the deliberate character of the act and bringing about a situation whereby subjectively there may not always be serious fault. But in general, the absence of serious responsibility must not be presumed; this would be to misunderstand people's moral capacity.[5]

Scripture makes no direct reference to masturbation, yet the Church has always regarded it to be a grave offense against chastity and an action not worthy of the dignity of the human person. Masturbation (especially when connected with the use of pornography) inverts a person's sex drive upon himself and can damage a person's ability to form real relationships and engage with others. It can become compulsive and addictive, enslaving the person in an unreal world of fantasy.

Pre-Marital Sex

Jesus Christ restored marriage to the original integrity it possessed before the Fall:

> "He answered, 'Have you not read that he who made them from the beginning made them male and female', and said, 'For this reason a man shall leave his father and mother and be joined to his wife, and the two shall become one flesh.' So they are no longer two but one flesh. What therefore God has joined together, let not man put asunder'" (Mt 19:4-6).

---

[4] *Catechism of the Catholic Church* #2352.
[5] *Persona Humana* #9.

Understanding the dignity of the person and the meaning of human sexuality, it becomes clear why the Church has always taught that sexual relations prior to marriage are gravely sinful.[6] Christ taught that sexual love between a man and a woman should exist only within the framework of a stable and permanent relationship free from whims and caprices. Only such a relationship can ensure the proper upbringing and education of children for God and the mutual help and companionship needed by each partner. The love between married people is an image of the love Christ has for His Church (Eph. 5:25-32), while pre-marital sex amounts to a desecration of the human body as the temple of the Holy Spirit:

> "Do you not know that your bodies are members of Christ? Should I therefore take the members of Christ and make them members of a prostitute? Never! Do you not know that whoever is united to a prostitute becomes one body with her? For it is said, The two shall be one flesh. But anyone united to the Lord becomes one spirit with him. Shun fornication! Every sin that a person commits is outside the body; but the fornicator sins against the body itself. Or do you not know that your body is a temple of the Holy Spirit within you, which you have from God, and that you are not your own? For you were bought with a price; therefore glorify God in your body" (1 Cor. 6:15-20).

Sex is the seal rather than the beginning of a relationship. The vows exchanged on the wedding day find their first fulfilment in the sexual union. Sex therefore *consummates*, elevating the male-female relationship to a sacred, covenantal plane. As a covenant, the marriage bond is indissoluble. This indissolubility 'protects' the sexual act to enable it to fulfil its procreative and unitive functions.

---

[6] Pope Innocent IV, *Sub Catholica Professione*, 1254; Pope Pius II, *Propos. Damn. in Ep. Cum Sicut Accepimus*, 1459; Decrees of the Holy Office, 1665 & 1679; Pope Pius XI, *Casti Connubii*, 1930.

Homosexuality

One of the criticisms lodged against the Church is that she does not accept homosexual persons. To this, two responses can be given. First, the Church as the Bride of Christ accepts and loves all people and specifically teaches that those with homosexual tendencies "must be accepted with respect, compassion and sensitivity."[7] Second, the Church refuses to label people as 'gay' or 'straight', teaching that,

> The human person, made in the image and likeness of God, can hardly be adequately described by a reductionist reference to his or her sexual orientation ... the Church ... refuses to consider the person as a "heterosexual" or a "homosexual" and insists that every person has a fundamental identity: the creature of God, and by grace, his child and heir to eternal life.[8]

The message that all people are created in the image of God is the foundation from which the Church teaches that homosexual actions are "intrinsically disordered." The sexual act has a meaning that cannot be changed according to preference or societal norms because it is called to reflect the very love of God. As homosexual actions are closed to the gift of life and lack a genuine sexual complementarity they can never be approved.[9] Consequently, the legalization of homosexual and lesbian 'marriages' can never be justified:

> Marriage is not just any relationship between human beings. It was established by the Creator with its own nature, essential properties and purpose. No ideology can erase from the human spirit the certainty that marriage exists solely between a man and a woman.[10]

---

[7] *Catechism of the Catholic Church* #2357.
[8] Sacred Congregation for the Doctrine of the Faith, *Letter to the Bishops of the Catholic Church on the Pastoral Care of Homosexual Persons*, 1986, #16.
[9] *Catechism of the Catholic Church* #2357.
[10] Sacred Congregation for the Doctrine of the Faith, *Considerations Regarding Proposals to give Legal Recognition to Unions between Homosexual Persons*, 2003, #2.

The Church understands that many people with same-sex attraction endure this inclination as a trial and a cross. The homosexual tendency is one of the varieties of disorders that people suffer in the post-Fall world. However, all people are called to perfection, to carry their particular cross and unite it with Christ's, something that can only be achieved with a resolute desire to live chastity and embrace the graces necessary to do so.

Pornography

Pornography has become a worldwide multi-billion dollar industry. It is readily available to all, including children, and in the privacy of our own homes.

Pornography is commonly defined as the depiction or portrayal of the human body with the intention of exciting sexual pleasure and lust. It may also involve the eroticization of violence, humiliation, degradation and other explicit forms of abuse.

Christians must resist the isolation and fragmentation that pornography represents. A sound theology of the body celebrates male and female physicality and recognizes that the body has a nuptial meaning ordered towards unity and new life.

The Catholic Church teaches that any association with pornography is a serious sin. "It does grave injury to the dignity of its participants (actors, vendors, the public), since each one becomes an object of base pleasure and illicit profit for others. It immerses all who are involved in the illusion of a fantasy world. It is a grave offense."[11]

To counter the scourge of pornography young people should be taught the value of avoiding occasions of temptation, modesty in dress, wholesome recreation, daily prayer, and frequent reception of the sacraments of Holy Communion and Confession.

---

[11] *Catechism of the Catholic Church* #2354.

The Fathers

St Justin Martyr, *Dialogue with Trypho* 5 (AD 155)

"These have conquered me - the divinity of the instruction, and the power of the Word: for as a skilled serpent-charmer lures the terrible reptile from his den and causes it to flee, so the Word drives the fearful passions of our sensual nature from the very recesses of the soul; first driving forth lust, through which every ill is begotten - hatreds, strife, envy, emulations, anger, and such like. Lust being once banished, the soul becomes calm and serene."

The Roman Catechism (1566)

Pt. III, Ch. VII: In the Gospel ... Christ the Lord says: *From the heart come forth adulteries and fornications, which defile a man.* The Apostle Paul expresses his detestation of this crime frequently, and in the strongest terms: *This is the will of God, your sanctification, that you should abstain from fornication; Fly fornication; Keep not company with fornicators; Fornication, and all uncleanness and covetousness, let it not so much as be named among you; Neither fornicators, nor adulterers, nor male prostitutes, nor sodomites shall possess the kingdom of God.*

Catechism of the Catholic Church (1992)

No. 2337: Chastity means the successful integration of sexuality within the person and thus the inner unity of man in his bodily and spiritual being. Sexuality, in which man's belonging to the bodily and biological world is expressed, becomes personal and truly human when it is integrated into the relationship of one person to another, in the complete and lifelong mutual gift of a man and a woman.

The virtue of chastity therefore involves the integrity of the person and the integrality of the gift.

Discussion Questions

1. Define chastity.

2. Why is masturbation viewed by the Church as a "seriously disordered act"?

3. Why should sexual intercourse always be within the context of a stable and permanent relationship?

4. Why can same-sex marriages never be justified?

5. How can homosexual persons achieve Christian perfection?

Activities

- Take some time to reflect upon chastity as providing an individual with freedom of choice in their life, rather than chastity as being a burden. Discuss and/or journal your responses.

- Discuss how pornography cheapens and exploits an individual's human dignity.

Transmission of Life

"I came that they may have life, and have it abundantly" (Jn 10:10).

The Gospel of Life

The Gospel of Life is at the heart of the message of the Church and is part of the "good news" that needs to be proclaimed and shared with the people of every age. Through its bodily existence, humanity is able to share in the very life of God, making all life of inestimable value. The Church firmly believes that every person open to truth and goodness can come to recognize the sacred value of each life from its earliest beginnings to its natural end. Furthermore, as if to increase the dignity of human life even further, the second person of the Blessed Trinity "was made flesh and dwelt amongst us" (Jn 1:14) in the person of Jesus, thus showing "the incomparable value of every human person."[1]

However, as humanity traverses the third millennium the Church and society faces its greatest challenge, an unprecedented "conspiracy against life" promoting a "culture of death"[2] affecting the whole realm of life and its transmission. This culture of death has rapidly enveloped broad sections of world public opinion to now justify and even promote various offenses against life in the name of individual freedom. The way in which life and relationships are valued and lived has been radically reconsidered. Even more serious is the fact that the human conscience has become darkened to such an extent that it is nigh impossible for society to distinguish between good and evil.[3] The culture of death finds in the Catholic Church its strongest opponent for she alone stands entirely against its declared agenda.

Contraception

The contraceptive mentality that has invaded the hearts and homes

---

[1] Pope St John Paul II, *Evangelium Vitae*, 1995, #2.
[2] Ibid. #17.
[3] Ibid. #4.

of the majority of the Western world (and increasingly the developing nations) lies at the foundation of the culture of death. When the fruit of sexual love is deliberately denied (even for what is considered just motives) the entire purpose of love is at risk.

> Such practices are rooted in a hedonistic mentality unwilling to accept responsibility in matters of sexuality, and they imply a self-centred concept of freedom, which regards procreation as an obstacle to personal fulfilment. The life which could result from a sexual encounter thus becomes an enemy to be avoided at all costs, and abortion becomes the only possible decisive response to failed contraception.[4]

From the pages of Sacred Scripture, the story of Onan in the Old Testament testifies to God's abhorrence of the marriage act being abused to avoid the procreation of children:

> *"Then Judah said to Onan, 'Go in to your brother's wife and perform the duty of a brother-in-law to her; raise up offspring for your brother.' But since Onan knew that the offspring would not be his, he spilled his semen on the ground whenever he went in to his brother's wife, so that he would not give offspring to his brother. What he did was displeasing in the sight of the Lord, and He put him to death ..."* (Gen. 38:8-10).

Until 1930, birth control of any kind was opposed by all religious bodies calling themselves Christian due to the belief that children are a great gift from God and that to separate the marital act from procreation directly opposed the Creator's plan for marriage. The Lambeth Conference of the Church of England in 1930 was the first to break from this position, justifying birth control provided it was practised "in the light of ... Christian principles and not from motives of selfishness, luxury or mere convenience." Since then, Protestantism as a whole has capitulated and no longer holds any moral objections to the use of birth control.

---

[4] *Ibid.* #13.

On the other hand, the Catholic Church since 1930 has maintained her opposition to all forms of contraception (condoms, intrauterine devices, the contraceptive pill, etc.):

> Any use of matrimony whatsoever in the exercise of which the marital act is deprived, by human interference, of its natural power to procreate life, is an offense against the law of God and of nature, and those who commit it are guilty of grave sin.[5]

> Any attempt on the part of the husband and wife to deprive this act of its inherent force or to impede the procreation of a new life, either in the performance of the act itself, or in the course of the development of its natural consequences, is immoral.[6]

> Relying on these principles, sons of the Church may not undertake methods of regulating procreation which are found blameworthy by the teaching authority of the Church.[7]

After the development of the contraceptive pill in 1960, the Church felt called to render a judgement as to its legitimacy. The long-awaited response was a re-affirmation of the Church's long-standing position against all forms of contraception:

> Similarly excluded is every action which, either in anticipation of the conjugal act, or in its accomplishment, or in the development of its natural consequences, proposes, whether as an end or as a means, to render procreation impossible.[8]

In the wake of this re-affirmation there followed a universal revolt both within and without the Catholic Church. This revolt was led tragically by some of the Church's leading theologians who argued that one's own private subjective conscience and not the Church's objective Magisterium should determine the licitness of contraceptive use:

---

[5] Pope Pius XI, *Casti Connubii*, 1930, #56.
[6] Pope Pius XII, *Address to Midwives*, 1951.
[7] Second Vatican Council, *Gaudium et Spes*, 1965, #51.
[8] Pope Paul VI, *Humanae Vitae*, 1968, #14.

When a Catholic Christian, after a mature examination of his conscience and with all possible self-criticism, thinks he can adopt a judgment that diverges from the papal norm and then follow this judgment in his own conjugal practice ... then a Catholic is not obliged to consider this a subjective sin nor is he to be regarded formally as one who is disobedient to ecclesial authority.[9]

It is not surprising that with such organized opposition, together with the wave of the 'sexual revolution' promoted by the world's media, approximately 80% to 90% of Catholics now use some form of artificial contraception. Nevertheless, the Church, as the herald of Christ and the Gospel, continues to make known the destructive nature of contraception, to both new life and the marital relationship:

> The Church has the mission of guarding the dignity of marriage and the transmission of life. And in regards to this latter, the teaching of *Humanae Vitae* is reaffirmed – contrary to the anti-life mentality which is so widespread at present.[10]

Sterilization

Another form of modern-day contraception equally prohibited by the Church is sterilization, either of the male or of the female. As with contraception, sterilization contradicts the full truth of the sexual act as the complete expression of marital love. There can be no distinction in the moral illicitness of using either the Pill, IUDs and sterilization:

> Equally to be excluded, as the teaching authority of the Church has frequently declared, is direct sterilization, whether perpetual or temporary, whether of the man or of the woman.[11]

---

[9] Karl Rahner, *Reflections on the Encyclical Humanae Vitae*, 1968.
[10] Pope St John Paul II, *Familiaris Consortio*, 1981, #29; Cf. *Veritatis Splendour*, 1993, #80; *Evangelium Vitae*, 1995, #13.
[11] *Humanae Vitae* #14; Cf. *Evangelium Vitae* ##3, 16 & 91.

Natural Family Planning

The immorality of contraception does not mean that every couple is called to have as many children as is biologically possible. While there is much generosity in having a large family, couples can confine the use of the marital act to infertile periods to limit or regulate their offspring where there exist "well grounded reasons" or motives. In all cases, a couple must truthfully put themselves before one another and God to discern how to organize their family:

> If, therefore, there are well-grounded reasons for spacing births, which derive from the physical or psychological conditions of husband and wife, or from external conditions, the Church teaches that it is then licit to take into account the natural rhythms immanent in the generative functions, for the use of marriage in the infecund periods only, and in this way to regulate birth without offending the moral principles which have been recalled earlier ... In reality, there are essential differences between the two cases: in the former, the married couple make legitimate use of a natural disposition; in the latter, they impede the development of natural processes.[12]

"Well grounded reasons" for using natural family planning would include grave economic hardship for the family as a whole, the transmission of genetic defects, or serious medical or psychological difficulties for the woman if she were to become pregnant. It is not legitimate, therefore, to engage in its use indiscriminately.

When a couple has recourse to the times of infertility instead of using contraception they uphold the honesty of the language of love. Instead of working against their fertility, they respect the unitive and procreative meanings of their sexuality and their moments of sexual union are integral without manipulation. The experience of such couples perceives the difference between contraception and the observation of a couples' natural fertility.

---

[12] *Ibid.* #16.

The choice of the natural rhythms involves accepting the cycle of the person, that is the woman, and thereby accepting dialogue, reciprocal respect, shared responsibility and self control. To accept the cycle and to enter in dialogue mean to recognize both the spiritual and corporal character of conjugal communion, and to live personal love with its requirement of fidelity. In this context the couple comes to experience how conjugal communion is enriched with those values of tenderness and affection which constitute the inner soul of human sexuality, in its physical dimension also. In this way sexuality is respected and promoted in its truly and fully human dimension, and is never "used" as an "object" that, by breaking the personal unity of soul and body, strikes at God's creation itself at the level of the deepest interaction of nature and person.[13]

---

[13] *Familiaris Consortio* #32; Cf. *Catechism of the Catholic Church* #2370.

The Fathers

Clement of Alexandria, *The Instructor of Children* 2, 10 (ante AD 202)
"Because of its divine institution for the propagation of man, the seed is not to be vainly ejaculated, nor is it to be damaged, nor is it to be wasted."

The Roman Catechism (1566)

Pt. II, Ch. VIII: A second reason for marriage is the desire of family, not so much, however, with a view to leave after us heirs to inherit our property and fortune, as to bring up children in the true faith and in the service of God ... It was also for this reason that God instituted marriage from the beginning; and therefore married persons who, to prevent conception or procure abortion, have recourse to medicine, are guilty of a most heinous crime ...

Catechism of the Catholic Church (1992)

No. 2367: Called to give life, spouses share in the creative power and fatherhood of God. Married couples should regard it as their proper mission to transmit human life and to educate their children; they should realise that they are thereby *cooperating with* the love of God the Creator and are, in a certain sense, its interpreters. They fulfill this duty with a sense of human and Christian responsibility.

No. 2373: Sacred Scripture and the Church's traditional practice see in large families a sign of God's blessing and the parents' generosity.

Discussion Questions

1. What is meant by the term 'culture of death'? Why should Christians be concerned?

2. Why does the Catholic Church oppose contraception?

3. Why is sterilization considered another form of contraception?

4. On what grounds can Christian couples use 'natural family planning'?

5. Why is natural family planning different from contraception?

Activities

- Look at the papal encyclical *Humanae Vitae* and write a brief statement about how this document respects the dignity of the human person.

- Outline some practical ways that might assist contemporary society to shift from being a 'culture of death' to a 'culture of life'.

Reproductive Technology

"For thou didst form my inward parts, thou didst knit me together in my mother's womb. I praise thee, for thou art fearful and wonderful" (Ps. 139:13-14).

Lord of all Life

At the dawn of creation, God the Creator and Father entrusted to humanity stewardship and dominion over all other living creatures (Gen. 1:26). Man and woman were invited to eat of all the fruits of the earth and use them for their benefit, except the fruit of the tree of the knowledge of good and evil from which they could not eat lest they die (Gen. 2:17 and 3:3). This tree reminds us that humanity is indeed free to choose and fashion but not free to create its own standards of right and wrong. God remains the supreme Creator and Lord of all life and we are called to employ the great gifts of intelligence and freedom for our own happiness under God's Lordship and grace.

When considering the increasingly complex issues of reproductive technology, it must be remembered that humanity is but a steward of life; God is the master of life. However, modern humanity too often forgets its limitations and easily moves to 'play God' in the realm of procreation and life:

> Thanks to the progress of the biological and medical sciences, man has at his disposal ever more effective therapeutic resources; but he can also acquire new powers, with unforeseeable consequences, over human life at its very beginning and in its first stages. Various procedures now make it possible to intervene not only in order to assist but also to dominate the processes of procreation. These techniques can enable man to take in hand his own destiny, but they also expose him to the temptation to go beyond the limits of a reasonable dominion over nature.[1]

---

[1] Congregation for the Doctrine of the Faith, *Donum Vitae*, 1980, Introduction, #1.

Modern-day Developments

Modern-day scientific developments have advanced to such an extent that it is now possible for couples to have children where it was previously naturally impossible. At first look, such developments appear to be at the service of life and contrary to the anti-life mentality. However, such techniques usually have no respect for the unique status of the embryo as a member of the human family and separate procreation from the marital act. Examples include in-vitro fertilization, artificial insemination, surrogate motherhood, cloning and embryo experimentation.

Science and technology have brought about many wonderful advances for humanity and they achieve this especially when they are placed at the service and development of all; however, it must be recognized that science cannot of itself discern what is moral from what is immoral. Just because a certain procedure *can* be done does not necessarily mean that it *should* be done. Thus, the Church makes clear that the field of science must have an "unconditional respect for the fundamental criteria of the moral law."[2] Furthermore,

> The transmission of human life is entrusted by nature to a personal and conscious act and as such is subject to the all-holy laws of God: immutable and inviolable laws which must be recognized and observed. For this reason one cannot use means and follow methods which could be licit in the transmission of the life of plants and animals.[3]

> Our era needs such wisdom more than in bygone ages if the discoveries made by man are to be further humanized. For the future of the world stands in peril unless wiser people are forthcoming.[4]

The Church has spoken clearly concerning various modern developments in reproductive technology. Again, when considering the

---

[2] *Donum Vitae*, Introduction, #2.
[3] *Ibid.* #4.
[4] Pope John Paul II, *Familiaris Consortio*, 1981, #8.

merit of techniques of artificial human procreation two values need always be considered: the unique life of the human being which is created in the image of God and the irreplaceable value of the transmission of life within marriage.

In-Vitro Fertilization (IVF)

> The various *techniques of artificial reproduction*, which would seem to be at the service of life and which are frequently used with this intention, actually open the door to new threats against life. Apart from the fact that they are morally unacceptable, since they separate procreation from the fully human context of the conjugal act, these techniques have a high rate of failure: not just failure in relation to fertilization but with regard to the subsequent development of the embryo, which is exposed to the risk of death, generally within a very short space of time. Furthermore, the number of the embryos produced is often greater than that needed for implantation in the woman's womb, and these so-called 'spare embryos' are then destroyed or used for research which, under the pretext of scientific or medical progress, in fact reduces human life to the level of simple biological material to be freely disposed of.[5]

While couples utilizing IVF may have good intentions (the birth of a child), one may never do an evil that a good might result. IVF is destructive of both the marital act and new life that is created. Technology may assist the sexual act to conceive new life but can never replace the sexual act. For human beings, the marital act is much more than just a biological process whereby sperm and egg are united; it is the union of man and woman in an act that is meant to unite them as one body. It is only from this unity that new life should be conceived. Furthermore, the destruction or freezing of many 'spare' living human embryos (on average 7-10 per IVF cycle) is the other side of the 'IVF coin', in which life and death are subjected to the arbitrary decisions of doctors who set themselves up as the givers of life and death.

---

[5] Pope St John Paul II, *Evangelium Vitae*, 1995, #14.

Artificial Insemination

Catholic teaching on human artificial insemination was first given summary attention by Pope Pius XII in 1949 in an address to Catholic physicians.[6] The Pope identified the following, among others, as moral concerns arising out of this procedure: the involvement of sperm from a third-party donor amounted to an invasion of the exclusive marriage covenant in a kind of mechanical adultery; the irresponsibility of the donor fathering a child for which he can fulfill no paternal function; and the donor's act of masturbation in order to thus donate his seed. In subsequent decades, the Church would also identify artificial insemination with a violation of the language of the human body:

> It is in their bodies and through their bodies that the spouses consummate their marriage and are able to become father and mother. In order to respect the language of their bodies and their natural generousity, the conjugal union must take place with respect for its openness to procreation; and the procreation of a person must be the fruit and the result of married love. The origin of the human being thus follows from a procreation that is "linked to the union, not only biological but also spiritual, of the parents, made one by the bond of marriage." Fertilization achieved outside the bodies of the couple remains by this very fact deprived of the meanings and the values which are expressed in the language of the body and in the union of human persons.[7]

The above teaching makes clear that, even if insemination could be artificially achieved with the husband's sperm properly collected without masturbation, any process that isolates the act of human generation from the marriage act itself is inconsistent with the holiness of the two-in-one-flesh union that alone is appropriate for the generation of children. As long, however, as the integrity of the marriage act is preserved, various medical techniques designed to facilitate the process of conception are not to be condemned.

---

[6] Pope Pius XII, Address to Catholic Physicians, September 29, 1949.
[7] *Donum Vitae*, Introduction, #2, B, (b).

Surrogate Motherhood

Surrogate motherhood involves both a violation of the sanctity of marriage and a violation of the rights of the child. It removes from the procreative process the mutual self-giving of the husband and wife intended by God and introduces a third party into the marriage. It removes love from the act of procreation.

> Surrogate motherhood represents an objective failure to meet the obligations of maternal love, of conjugal fidelity and of responsible motherhood; it offends the dignity and the right of the child to be conceived, carried in the womb, brought into the world and brought up by his own parents; it sets up, to the detriment of families, a division between the physical, psychological and moral elements which constitute those families.[8]

In traditional surrogacy, fertilization is achieved in a petri dish. Six to eight embryos are usually quick-frozen and stored in a laboratory for future use. Later, two or more of the embryos are implanted, at the appropriate time of the cycle, in the third-party uterus. The foetuses develop and if more than one is viable the 'extra foetuses' may be removed. This process is called 'selective reduction'; in reality, this is abortion, the termination of the 'extra' foetuses. The surviving foetus then hopefully grows to term in the third-party uterus.

Artificial insemination does violence to the dignity of the human person. It separates the sexual act from the procreative act. The act that brings the child into existence is no longer one by which two persons give themselves to one another, but one that "entrusts the life and identity of the embryo into the power of doctors and biologists and establishes the domination of technology over the origin and destiny of the human person."[9]

---

[8] *Donum Vitae*, Introduction, #2, A, 3.
[9] *Catechism of the Catholic Church* #2377.

Cloning and Embryo Experimentation

What about research on a human embryo?

These procedures are contrary to the human dignity proper to the embryo, and at the same time they are contrary to the right of every person to be conceived and to be born within marriage and from marriage. Also, attempts or hypotheses for obtaining a human being without any connection with sexuality through "twin fission", cloning or parthenogenesis are to be considered contrary to the moral law, since they are in opposition to the dignity both of human procreation and of the conjugal union.

The freezing of embryos, even when carried out in order to preserve the life of an embryo - cryopreservation - constitutes an offense against the respect due to human beings by exposing them to grave risks of death or harm to their physical integrity and depriving them, at least temporarily, of maternal shelter and gestation, thus placing them in a situation in which further offenses and manipulation are possible.

Certain attempts to influence chromosomic or genetic inheritance are not therapeutic but are aimed at producing human beings selected according to sex or other predetermined qualities. These manipulations are contrary to the personal dignity of the human being and his or her integrity and identity.[10]

The Church teaches that medical research must refrain from operations on live embryos, unless there is moral certainty of not causing harm to the life or integrity of the unborn child and mother, and on condition that the parents have given free and informed consent to the procedure. Furthermore, as children are essentially gifts from God no one has a right to tamper with an embryo. No person or couple can demand or claim an entitlement to a child; it is a privilege granted by God. Children are not commodities that can be bought or altered at the discretion of others.

In responding to the pain of couples who are having difficulty conceiving, one recent breakthrough has been made by the *Paul VI*

---

[10] *Donum Vitae*, Introduction, #1, 6.

Institute for the Study of Human Reproduction. A greater understanding of the human reproductive system has seen the development of 'Napro-Technology' which helps a couple analyze the data of their own fertility to discover and treat whatever is preventing them from conceiving. 'NaproTech' has seen great success in treating many who have told even by IVF doctors that they would never conceive.

The Fathers

The Fathers, for obvious reasons, made no reference to the issue of reproductive technology.

The Roman Catechism (1566)

The Roman Catechism likewise made no reference to the issue of reproductive technology.

Catechism of the Catholic Church (1992)

No. 2274: Since it must be treated from conception as a person, the embryo must be defended in its integrity, cared for, and healed, as far as possible, like any other human being.

> *Prenatal diagnosis* is morally licit, "if it respects the life and integrity of the embryo and the human fetus and is directed toward its safe guarding or healing as an individual ... It is gravely opposed to the moral law when this is done with the thought of possibly inducing an abortion, depending upon the results: a diagnosis must not be the equivalent of a death sentence."

No. 2275: One must hold as licit procedures carried out on the human embryo which respect the life and integrity of the embryo and do not involve disproportionate risks for it, but are directed toward its healing, the improvement of its condition of health, or its individual survival.

It is immoral to produce human embryos intended for exploitation as disposable biological material.

No. 2375: Research aimed at reducing human sterility is to be encouraged, on condition that it is placed "at the service of the human person, of his inalienable rights, and his true and integral good according to the design and will of God."

Discussion Questions

1. In what ways can modern-day developments in reproductive technology appear to be pro-life?

2. What two values must always be considered when evaluating the merits of reproductive technology?

3. List some reasons why the Catholic Church opposes in-vitro fertilization.

4. List some reasons why the Catholic Church opposes surrogacy.

5. How can 'Napro-Technology' assist couples who experience difficulties conceiving children?

Activities

- In November, 2001, a woman named Renee Shields lost her unborn son, Byron, after an incident of road rage. This has led to 'Byron's Law', a law designed to protect pregnant mothers and their unborn children.
- Investigate 'Byron's Law'. How does this law recognize the integrity of the human person? At what stage of development should the rights of the unborn child be recognized?

Ethics of Life & Death

"It is I who bring forth death and life" (Deut. 32:39).

Abortion

From Scripture it is clear that God regards the child in the mother's womb as already a human being in the full sense with a life protected by the commandment "Thou shalt not kill":

"For thou didst form my inward parts, thou didst knit me together in my mother's womb" (Ps. 139:13).

"Now the word of the Lord came to me saying, 'Before I formed you in the womb I knew you, and before you were born I consecrated you; I appointed you a prophet to the nations'" (Jer. 1:4-5).

"When Elizabeth heard Mary's greeting, the child leaped in her womb. And Elizabeth was filled with the Holy Spirit and exclaimed with a loud cry, 'Blessed are you among women, and blessed is the fruit of your womb. And why has this happened to me, that the mother of my Lord comes to me?'" (Lk 1:41-42).

Abortion has always been vigorously opposed by the Church as a sin against the goodness of life.[1] While Western societies during the twentieth century generally moved to accept abortion as a 'woman's right', the Church continued to proclaim its total opposition:

From the moment of its conception life must be guarded with the greatest care, while abortion and infanticide are unspeakable crimes.[2]

Above all, directly willed and procured abortion, even for therapeutic reasons, is to be absolutely excluded.[3]

---

[1] Pope Stephen V, *Consuluisti de Infantibus*, 891 (DS 670); Decr. *Sancti Officii*, 1679 (DS 2134-5); *Responsa Sancti Officii*, 1895 (DS 3298).
[2] Second Vatican Council, *Gaudium et Spes*, 1965, #51.
[3] Pope Paul VI, *Humanae Vitae*, 1968, #14.

We declare that direct abortion, that is, abortion willed as an end or as a means, always constitutes a grave moral disorder, since it is the deliberate killing of an innocent human being. This doctrine is based upon the written Word of God, is transmitted by the Church's Tradition and taught by the ordinary and universal magisterium.[4]

In more recent times, Pope Benedict XVI has added his voice to the debate, noting that abortion is a form of aggression that attacks both the individual and the broader society:

(I)t is necessary to help all people to be aware that the intrinsic evil of the crime of abortion, which attacks human life at its beginning, is also an aggression against society itself.[5]

With advances in scientific and medical technology, it is now easy to access and observe the developmental stages of a child from conception through to birth. It is, therefore, no longer possible to claim that the unborn child is not a human being. Consequently, the debate has been narrowed to a matter of 'choice.' Often a woman may feel that in her particular circumstances she has no choice but to abort her child; however, it is precisely in such moments that the natural father of the child, the wider family, society and the Church must be present to offer support to both the mother and her unborn baby and provide viable alternatives to abortion.

Infanticide

Directly flowing from the abortion mentality is the growing acceptance of infanticide. In China alone, due to its recently abandoned one-child policy and cultural preference for males, more than six hundred thousand cases of infanticide were committed against infant females each year. At the same time, certain voices are calling for infanticide to be available as a right to Western parents:

---

[4] Pope St John Paul II, *Evangelium Vitae*, 1995, #62.
[5] Pope Benedict XVI, *Address to the presidents of Latin American bishops' committees for the family and for life*, 4 December, 2005.

In our book, *Should the Baby Live?*, ... I suggested that a period of twenty-eight days after birth might be allowed before an infant is accepted as having the same right to life as others. This is clearly well before the infant could have a sense of its own existence over time, and would allow a couple to decide that it is better not to continue with a life that has begun very badly.[6]

The Church is watchful of these developments and has in recent years stated:

> The contemporary scene, moreover, is becoming even more alarming by reason of the proposals, advanced here and there, to justify even *infanticide*, following the same arguments used to justify the right to abortion. In this way, we revert to a state of barbarism which one hoped had been left behind forever.[7]

Euthanasia

The ever-increasing technological advance of Western society since the Industrial Revolution has given rise to a determined effort to secure man's control over all aspects of his existence. Having wiped God from his mind, modern man places himself upon the pedestal as the supreme lord of life and death. Only his own creative genius limits his dominion.

Man has usurped control over the creation of new life through contraception and abortion; in order to usurp control over death the social revolutionaries now clamor for the legalization of euthanasia.

Contraception, abortion and euthanasia are fruits of the same anti-life mentality.

Euthanasia is any act or omission which of itself and by intention causes death with the purpose of eliminating all suffering.[8] It is the moral equivalent of suicide and hence a sin against the fifth commandment, *Thou shall not kill*. Its proponents often masquerade it under euphemistic

---

[6] Peter Singer, *Rethinking Life and Death*, The Text Publishing Co., Melbourne, 1993, p. 217.
[7] *Evangelium Vitae* #14.
[8] Sacred Congregation for the Doctrine of the Faith, *Declaration on Euthanasia*, 1980.

terms such as 'mercy-killing', 'self-delivery' or 'dying with dignity.' Many qualifiers are often attached to the word, such as active or passive, negative or positive, voluntary or involuntary.

These slogans are devised to gradually caress public opinion into accepting euthanasia. Advocates of euthanasia are increasingly demanding the right to exercise the following:

(i) To support the conscious demands of individuals with irreparable disabilities or degenerative diseases to terminate their lives even though natural death is not imminent.
(ii) To deny everyday sustenance (food and drink) to unconscious terminally ill patients or patients on life support with little to no hope of recovery.
(iii) To abstain from having recourse to ordinary means of medical treatment available to save or prolong the lives of terminally ill patients or children with congenital defects or grave deformities.
(iv) To allow for the compulsory elimination of all those who constitute an economic burden to society.

In May 1995, the Government of the Northern Territory of Australia became the first in the world to tread down this path by passing the "Rights of the Terminally Ill Bill." This law came into effect on 1 July 1996 but was revoked by overriding Federal legislation in March 1997. In April 2001 the Dutch parliament legalized euthanasia, ominously preparing the way for the rest of Europe to follow. The debate over euthanasia continues to rage in all state, territorial and federal parliaments across Australia.

Due to advancements in palliative care, the 'need' for euthanasia legislation is actually decreasing rather than increasing. There are now very few cases where a patient's medical and nursing needs cannot be adequately catered for. Legitimate 'dying with dignity' guidelines, when followed, are so sophisticated that in most cases pain and suffering are no longer a significant problem. 'Euthanasiasts' advocate removing suffering not by practical charity and assistance, but by death.

The alleged chief aim of euthanasiasts is the elimination of all prolonged pain and suffering. Yet, in the eyes of the Christian, pain and suffering can have a purifying and meritorious value:

... suffering, especially during the last moments of life, has a special place in God's saving plan; it is in fact a sharing in Christ's Passion and a union with the redeeming sacrifice which he offered in obedience to the Father's will. Therefore one must not be surprised if some Christians prefer to moderate their use of painkillers, in order to accept voluntarily at least part of their sufferings and thus associate themselves in a conscious way with the sufferings of Christ crucified (cf. Mt 27:34).[9]

Coinciding with renewed legislative attempts to legalize euthanasia, Pope St John Paul II re-stated the Church's traditional moral objection:

> ... in harmony with the Magisterium of my predecessors and in communion with the Bishops of the Catholic Church, we confirm that euthanasia is a grave violation of the law of God, since it is the deliberate and morally unacceptable killing of a human person. This doctrine is based upon the natural law and upon the written word of God, is transmitted by the Church's Tradition and taught by the ordinary and universal Magisterium.[10]

Furthermore, the Holy Father made the following observations:

> (E)uthanasia must be called a false mercy, and indeed a disturbing 'perversion of mercy.' True 'compassion' leads to sharing another's pain; it does not kill the person whose suffering we cannot bear. Moreover, the act of euthanasia appears all the more perverse if it is carried out by those, like relatives, who are supposed to treat a family member with patience and love, or by those, such as doctors who by virtue of their specific profession are supposed to care for the sick person even in the most painful terminal stages ... Once again we find ourselves before the temptation of Eden: to become like God who 'knows good and evil' (cf. Gen. 3:5). God alone has the power over life and death: 'It is I who bring forth death and life'

---

[9] *Declaration on Euthanasia* III.
[10] *Evangelium Vitae* #65.

(Dt 32:39; cf. 2 Kgs 5:7; 1 Sam. 2:6) ... when man usurps this power, being enslaved by a foolish and selfish way of thinking, he inevitably uses it for injustice and death.[11]

As a final point, what of the passive omission or removal of 'extraordinary means' of preserving a person's life? 'Extraordinary means' usually include medical treatments that are overly expensive, burdensome and offer no hope of recovery. In such circumstances, the removal of extraordinary means does not amount to euthanasia and is morally permissible in the eyes of the Church. Once a patient has irreversibly entered the dying process it is permissible to limit medical treatment to the provision of ordinary means and everyday sustenance and allow natural processes to take their course.[12]

---

[11] *Evangelium Vitae* #66.
[12] *Catechism of the Catholic Church* #2278.

The Fathers

The Didache 2, 1 (inter AD 90-150)

"The second commandment of the teaching: You shall not murder. You shall not commit adultery. You shall not seduce boys. You shall not commit fornication. You shall not steal. You shall not practise magic. You shall not use potions. You shall not procure abortion, nor destroy a newborn child. You shall not bear false witness. You shall not speak evil. You shall not bear malice."

The Roman Catechism (1566)

Pt. III, Ch. VI: No man possesses such power over his own life as to be at liberty to put himself to death. Hence we find that the Commandment does not say: *Thou shalt not kill another*, but simply: *Thou shalt not kill.*

Catechism of the Catholic Church (1992)

No. 2277: Whatever its motives and means, direct euthanasia consists in putting an end to the lives of handicapped, sick, or dying persons. It is morally unacceptable ... Thus an act or omission which, of itself or by intention, causes death in order to eliminate suffering constitutes a murder gravely contrary to the dignity of the human person and to the respect due to the living God, his Creator. The error of judgment into which one can fall in good faith does not change the nature of this murderous act, which must always be forbidden and excluded.

No. 2279: Even if death is thought imminent, the ordinary care owed to a sick person cannot be legitimately interrupted. The use of painkillers to alleviate the sufferings of the dying, even at the risk of shortening their days, can be morally in conformity with human dignity if death is not willed as either an end or a means, but only foreseen and tolerated as inevitable. Palliative care is a special form of disinterested charity. As such it should be encouraged.

Discussion Questions

1. Abortion violates which of the Ten Commandments?

2. When must respect for human life begin?

3. How should one advise a woman contemplating an abortion?

4. Why are female children more often the victims of infanticide?

5. What legitimate alternatives exist to euthanasia?

Activities

- Find examples of how the media presents the issues of abortion and euthanasia. How does this compare with the Catholic view of life and death?
- Brainstorm and consider all those who would be affected by a choice to end life. For example, how would doctors and nurses be affected by an individual who considers ending their life?
- Investigate the role of a geriatrician. Why is palliative care the preferred Catholic response for those individuals who have a terminal illness?

Prayers

Prayer for Purity

Lord Jesus,
I praise you and thank you for the gift of my sexuality.
By the power of your death and resurrection, heal in me what sin has wounded so that I might experience love, marriage and sexual desire as you intended, namely, *freely, totally, faithfully,* and *fruitfully.*
Amen.

Prayers for a Good Spouse

Lord Jesus,
Lover of the young, I open my heart to you and ask your assistance in the important task of planning my future. Give me the light of your grace that I may decide wisely concerning the person whom I should marry. Bless our friendship before marriage, that sin may have no part. May our mutual love bind us closely and may our future home reflect that of yours in Nazareth.
Amen.

O Mary Immaculate,
Dear Mother of the young, to your special care I entrust the decision I am to make as to my future spouse. You are my guiding Star! Direct me to the person with whom I can best cooperate in doing God's will, with whom I can live in peace, love and harmony in this life, and attain to eternal happiness in the next.
Amen.

Prayer of an Engaged Couple

Lord Jesus,
You have desired that [name] and I should live as one in you. Let our love realise a perfect union, not only of our hearts but also of our souls, growing from day to day. Bring to our future home children, health, thrift, purity, strength, and ideals, to make it a model of the new world we wish to build with you.
Amen.

Prayer for Marriage

Lord Jesus,
We thank you for the love you have implanted in our hearts.
May it always inspire us to be kind in our words, considerate of feeling, and concerned for each other's needs and wishes. Help us to be understanding and forgiving of human weaknesses and failings. Increase our faith and trust in you and may your grace
guide our lives and love.
Amen.

Married Couple's Prayer

Lord Jesus,
May we always treasure the experience of loving each other in this holy union. Help us to remain forever committed to our vows, those we made to each other, and to you. May we love each other with patience, respect, understanding, honesty, forgiveness and kindness. Let us always be a support to one another – a friend to listen and encourage, a refuge from the storms, and a partner in prayer.
Holy Spirit, guide us through the difficult moments of life and comfort us in our grief. May our lives together bring glory to you, our Savior, and testify to your love.
Amen.

Appendix

Prayer for Families

Heavenly Father,
Help us to live as the Holy Family did, united in respect and love. Bless and make holy all human love, especially the life-giving love of husband and wife. May your love fill the hearts and homes of all families, so that the world may enjoy the peace and happiness promised by your Son, our Lord Jesus Christ.
Amen.

Prayer to be a Good Parent

O God our Father,
You have given me children and committed them to my care to raise them up for you and to prepare them for eternal life. Help me that I may be able to fulfill this sacred duty and stewardship. Teach me to give and to withhold, to correct and to forbear, to be gentle and firm, and to be considerate and watchful. May I be careful to lead them in the ways of wisdom and piety, so that I may, with them, be admitted to the joys of our true home in heaven.
Amen.

Parents' Prayer for their Children

Heavenly Father,
I commend my children to your care. Be their true Father and supply whatever is lacking in my stewardship. Strengthen them to overcome whatever temptations they may encounter. Infuse your grace into their hearts and strengthen in them the gifts of your Holy Spirit so they may grow in grace and in the knowledge of Jesus Christ; and so, faithfully serving you here, they may come to rejoice in your presence hereafter.
Amen.

Internet Resources

Life, Marriage and Family Office Archdiocese of Melbourne:

www.cam.org.au/lifemarriagefamily/

Life, Marriage and Family Centre Archdiocese of Sydney YouTube video channel and website:

www.youtube.com/user/LifeMarriageFamily

www.lifemarriagefamily.org.au/

Catholic Marriage – An initiative of the United States Conference of Catholic Bishops:

http://foryourmarriage.org/

Christopher West on Theology of the Body, Marriage Preparation and Adult Faith Formation:

www.christopherwest.com/page.asp?ContentID=121

Theology of the Body for Teens:

http://thetheologyofthebody.com/information/teens

Homosexuality – Courage:

www.couragerc.net/

NaPro Technology:

www.fertilitycare.com.au/?page_id=7

Marriage and Family:

www.marriagepreparation.com/Links.htm

Appendix

Glossary

Adultery
Sexual intercourse committed by a married person with one who is not his or her spouse.

Annulment
The declaration by a Church tribunal that a marriage was never validly formed.

Artificial Insemination
A procedure in which a fine catheter tube is inserted through the cervix into the uterus to deposit a sperm sample directly into the uterus. The purpose of this procedure is to achieve pregnancy.

Blessing
A prayer that invokes God's power and care upon a person, place, thing or undertaking, accompanied usually with the sign of the cross.

Catechism of the Catholic Church
Published in 1992, the official statement of the Church's faith and of Catholic doctrine. Pope St John Paul II declared it to be a "sure norm for teaching the faith."

Catholic
A word of Greek origin meaning universal. The Church is Catholic because she possesses the fullness of Christ's presence, teachings and means of salvation, and because she has been sent out to convert the whole human race.

Celibacy
The chosen state of a person who wishes to abstain from all sexual intercourse with the intention of giving oneself totally to God.

Chastity
The moral virtue of self-control and purity in sexual matters.

Cloning
The technique of producing a genetically identical copy of an organism by replacing the nucleus of an unfertilized ovum with the nucleus of a body cell from the organism.

Communion of Persons (*communio personarum*)
Humans are social beings and need to relate to others to properly live and develop their potential.

Concupiscence
The wound in human nature caused by original sin that leads to disordered desire for bodily pleasure.

Conscience
The judgment of the human intellect concerning the morality of an act that has been done, is being done, or is to be done in the future.

Contraception
Any use of mechanical, chemical or medical procedures before, during or after sexual intercourse to prevent the conception of new human life.

Covenant
A solemn agreement between God and his people or between human beings involving mutual commitments or guarantees. The Scriptures speak of God entering into covenants with Adam, Noah, Abraham, Moses and David. Christ inaugurated the "new and everlasting covenant." Marriage is also a covenant.

Decalogue
Literally translated as the "ten words." Commonly known as the Ten Commandments, given by God to Moses for the moral and religious welfare of the Hebrew, or Chosen, People (Exod. 20:1-17).

Divorce
The termination of a lawful marriage before the death of either spouse.

Doctrine
The revealed or applied teachings of Christ as taught officially by the Church.

Dogma
A truth formally and solemnly declared by the Church to have been revealed by God, and thus to be believed by all. Dogmas are irreformable.

Domestic Church
The extent to which the Christian family accepts the Gospel and matures in faith it becomes an evangelizing community. The Christian family is called upon, by its example and witness, to enlighten all those who seek the truth.

Euthanasia
Euthanasia is any act or omission which of itself and by intention causes death with the purpose of eliminating all suffering.

Examination of Conscience
Prayerful reflection on our thoughts, words, deeds and omissions to determine if and how we have lived our lives in relation to the will of God. This practice is an important element in preparing to receive the sacrament of Penance.

Fathers of the Church
Eighty six men (forty-nine Greek and thirty-seven Latin) recognized by the Church for their extraordinary written contributions to the development of Christian doctrine in the period between AD 80 and AD 749.

Fornication
Sexual intercourse between a man and a woman who are both unmarried.

Grace, actual
A transient Divine help given at a specific time, often in answer to prayer, to enlighten the intellect and strengthen the will so to enable one to do the will of God.

Grace, sanctifying
The created participation in the life of God, making us temples of the Holy Spirit, adopted children of the Father and heirs to the Kingdom. It is first granted in Baptism and enriched or restored in the other sacraments and through prayer and good works.

Heaven
The state of eternal life with God, the communion of life and love with the Trinity and all the blessed, of supreme and definitive happiness, given to those who die in God's grace and friendship and are perfectly purified of their sins.

Hell
The state of eternal separation from God and suffering, reserved for those who refuse by their own free choice to believe and repent of their sins at the moment of death. The most acute suffering for those in hell is the 'pain of loss', that is, the realization that one has forfeited the vision of God for eternity.

Holiness
The state of the soul consisting in great love for God and neighbor and the commitment to do God's will. Also called sanctity. People who attain a heroic degree of holiness are called "saints."

Homosexuality
Sexual attraction towards another of the same sex.

Image of God (Imago Dei)
Each person is created in the image of God due to the spiritual gifts of intellect (power to understand) and will (power to love). Each and every person's personal dignity is based upon being created in the image of God.

Infanticide
The deliberate killing of a newly born child.

In-vitro Fertilization (IVF)
A laboratory procedure in which sperm is placed with an unfertilized egg in a Petri dish to achieve fertilization. The embryo is then transferred into the uterus to begin a pregnancy or frozen for future use.

Lust
Disordered desire for or enjoyment of sexual pleasure for its own sake separate and apart from marital love.

Marriage
The relationship established by God in which a man and woman freely consent to unite together in a life-long covenant.

Masturbation
The deliberate act of exciting one's own genitals to obtain sexual pleasure.

Model of faith
A person who is deeply committed to living out the Gospel and is an example for others. Everyday models of faith include good parents, teachers and catechists and all holy faith-filled people.

Mortal sin
A serious sin committed with full knowledge and consent that kills the life of grace and, if unrepented, will lead to eternal separation from God.

Natural Family Planning
A technique of family planning that relies on knowledge of the woman's fertility cycle rather than artificial contraceptives. Approved by the Church where there are "well-grounded reasons" for spacing or limiting births.

New Commandment
The commandment of charity given by Jesus Christ at the Last Supper to "Love one another, just as I have loved you" (Jn 13:34). Jesus explicitly stated that this would be the special sign of his followers.

Nuptial Blessing
Prayers said for the blessing of a couple during their wedding, especially of the bride.

Original Sin
The sin by which our first parents wilfully disobeyed the commandment of God, choosing to follow their own will rather than the will of God. The term also applies to the fallen state of human nature which affects all humanity and which is remitted through Baptism.

Penance
Interior penance is a conversion of heart towards God and a turning away from sin, with the intention of changing one's life. External acts of penance include fasting, prayer, and almsgiving.

Penitent
A person who repents of sin and seeks forgiveness and is willing to undertake whatever penances the Church prescribes.

Personal sin
An individual's deliberate and wilful choice to offend God by a thought, word, deed or omission.

Pornography
The depiction or portrayal of the human body with the intention of exciting sexual pleasure and lust.

Radical Feminism
An anti-Christian and naturalistic movement that advocates 'uni-sexism' and the final abolition of all remaining legal and cultural distinctions between men and women. It rigorously defends universal birth control, abortion on demand, free and easy divorce procedures, homosexuality, etc.

Reconciliation
The sacrament, also known as the sacrament of Penance, in which a person who has confessed his or her sins is forgiven by the priest and is

reconciled with God and the Church.

Repentance
Turning away and saying sorry to God for one's sins, with the sincere intention of trying to avoid sin in the future.

Sacrament
An external rite with outward or visible signs instituted by Jesus Christ that confers grace on the recipient(s). The seven sacraments are: Baptism, Confirmation, Eucharist, Penance, Anointing of the Sick, Holy Orders and Matrimony

Saint
In the New Testament, any Christian person living in a state of grace. The term is commonly reserved for those who have been officially recognized by the Church as holy in a process called canonization. Every person in heaven is a saint.

Salvation
The forgiveness of sins and restoration of friendship with God through Jesus Christ, leading to eternal life in heaven.

Sin
A deliberate thought, word, deed or omission contrary to the law of God.

Sterilization
Any procedure, medical or otherwise, carried out on a male or female with the intention of rendering that person incapable (permanently or temporarily) of conceiving a child.

Surrogate Mother
A woman who bears a child for another person, often for pay, either through artificial insemination or by carrying until birth another woman's surgically implanted fertilized egg.

Theology
The study of God and matters relating to God. From the Greek words

Theos (God) and Logos (word).

Theology of the Body
The series of one hundred and twenty-nine lectures delivered by Pope St John Paul II relating to the Divine plan for human love and the body during his Wednesday audiences between September 1979 and November 1984.

Virginity
The chosen state of a person who has never engaged in sexual activity and who wishes to continue abstaining from all sexual intercourse with the intention of giving oneself totally to God.

Virtue
An acquired or infused good habit that helps us to do good and avoid evil. The virtues include faith, hope and charity (theological virtues) and prudence, justice, fortitude and temperance (cardinal virtues).

Vocation
A calling from God to carry out his will in a particular way, e.g., in the religious life, priesthood, marriage, etc. The reward for fidelity to one's vocation is eternal life.

Vow
A deliberate and formal promise made to God.

Will of God
The plan that God has for every human person. The reward for fulfilling God's will is eternal life.

Special Thanks ...

The following persons deserve a special mention for the assistance provided towards the production of this book:

Louise Zavone: for her assistance in drafting the activities at the end of each chapter.

Anthony Cleary: for his moral support and providing staff to review the draft text and activities.

Fr Anthony Percy: for giving his time to examine the original draft and suggesting many detailed and beneficial changes.

Fr Peter Joseph: for his generosity in making two detailed examinations of the entire text.

Paul Mooney: for his wonderful work in producing the cover of this book.

About the Authors ...

Robert Haddad holds qualifications in law, theology, philosophy and religious education, namely, a LL.B, Grad. Cert. in RE, Grad. Dip. Ed., Grad. Dip. in Teacher Ed., MA (Theo. Studies), MRelEd, M. Phil. and AML (Oxon.). Robert has authored various books, including *Lord of History Series* and *Christ the Teacher Series, Defend the Faith!, The Case for Christianity – St Justin Martyr's Arguments for Religious Liberty and Judicial Justice*, and most recently edited and contributed to *Answering the Anti-Catholic Challenge*.

From 2006-2008 Robert headed the Catholic Chaplaincy at the University of Sydney. He also lectured at the Center for Thomistic Studies from 1996-2008, teaching Apologetics, Church Fathers and Church History, and assisted part-time with *Lumen Verum Apologetics*. From 2009-2012, Robert was the Director of the Confraternity of Christian Doctrine (Sydney) and in that capacity was the chief editor of the revised *Christ our Light and Life* (3rd Edition) religious education K-12 curriculum used by Catholic students in state schools as well as the *Gratia Series* sacramental programs for children preparing for Reconciliation, First Holy Communion, and Confirmation in the Archdiocese of Sydney. Currently, Robert is the Head of New Evangelization for the Catholic Education Office (Sydney) and lectures in Theology at the University of Notre Dame, Sydney.

Bernard Toutounji – After spending a number of years in undergraduate theological study and discernment of a priestly vocation in Sydney, Bernard moved to Melbourne to undertake a Master of Theology in Marriage and Family Studies at the *John Paul II Institute for Marriage and the Family*. At the completion of this course, Bernard returned to Sydney to work on the Liturgies for World Youth Day 2008. Since 2009, Bernard has worked as the Education Officer of the *Life, Marriage and Family Centre* of the Catholic Archdiocese of Sydney. He is a sessional tutor in theology at the University of Notre Dame and Campion College. He has a particular interest in moral theology and Pope John Paul's Theology of the Body. He writes and speaks on these topics and also attends intensive courses at the *Theology of the Body Institute* in the USA.

www.ingramcontent.com/pod-product-compliance
Lightning Source LLC
Chambersburg PA
CBHW071536080526
44588CB00011B/1687